THE FRENCH SAS IN HOLLAND

OPERATION 'AMHERST', THE LAST AIRBORNE OPERATION OF WW2

THEN AND NOW

THE FRENCH SAS IN HOLLAND

OPERATION 'AMHERST', THE LAST AIRBORNE OPERATION OF WW2

THEN AND NOW

By Karel Margry

AFTER THE BATTLE

An Imprint of Pen & Sword Books Ltd

The French SAS in Holland
Operation 'Amherst', the Last Airborne Operation of WW2 – Then and Now

Published by After the Battle
An imprint of Pen & Sword Books Ltd
Yorkshire – Philadelphia
Email: enquiries@pen-and-sword.co.uk
Website: **www.afterthebattle.com • www.pen-and-sword.co.uk**

ISBN: 978-1-03618-327-1

Commissioning Editor: Martin Mace
Design: Paul Wilkinson
Cover design: Jon Wilkinson
Printed and bound in India by Replika Press Pvt. Ltd.

Credits:
This book is a greatly expanded version of an article by the same author titled 'Operation 'Amherst'. French SAS in Holland, 1945' previously published in *After the Battle* magazine, issue 185 (August 2019).

Acknowledgements:
The author would like to thank Wybo Boersma, Johan van Doorn, Jannie Hadderingh, Willem van Hemmen, André Jans, Erik Jellema, Harold de Jong, Dennis Mijeringh, Joël Stoppels and Harry Venema.

Photo Credit Abbreviations:
ECPAD – Médiathèque de la Défense, Fort d'Ivry. LAC – Library and Archives Canada. Unless specified otherwise, all illustrations are from the After the Battle archive.

Front Cover:
Stick No. 11 of the 2ème RCP commanded by Aspirant Marcel Edmé, pictured at RAF Great Dunmow in the late afternoon of April 7, 1945, shortly before their take-off for Holland in Operation 'Amherst'. (ECPAD)

Back Cover:
Top: Two armoured Jeeps of the 5th (Belgian) SAS, pictured at the farm of the Pol family on the north bank of the Oranjekanaal near Orvelte, where they arrived on April 11 and relieved several sticks of the 2ème RCP holding out in the Schoonloo woods – then and now. (Wybo Boersma Collection)

Centre: German prisoners of war, taken by troops of the 2ème RCP in the preceding days, being marched through the village of Rolde after the French parachutists linked up with Canadian ground troops on April 12 – then and now.(ECPAD/Karel Margry)

Bottom: Members of stick No. 14 of the 3ème RCP commanded by Lieutenant Pierre Baratin posing with local Dutch girls at De Star windmill at Balkbrug in the southern part of the 'Amherst' area – then and now. (Wybo Boersma Collection/Karel Margry)

Frontispiece:
French SAS troops at Mushroom Farm Camp preparing to leave for their take-off airfields for Operation 'Amherst' on April 7, 1945.

MIX
Paper | Supporting responsible forestry
FSC™ C016779
FSC www.fsc.org

CONTENTS

The stick of Lieutenant Jean Appriou of the 2ème Régiment de Chasseurs Parachutistes (4th SAS), pictured in the woods west of the village of Gasselte. (ECPAD CTT-14-322)

INTRODUCTION

BY THE FIRST WEEK of April 1945 the Second World War in Europe was not over yet but rapidly approaching its inevitable end.

On the Eastern Front, the Soviet Red Army had started its Vistula–Oder offensive on January 12, attacking on a broad front with five army groups, and after three weeks of spectacular progress right across Poland had reached the Oder river, the last major obstacle before Berlin, in early February. Hard battles had been fought for the city of Poznan, the last bastion before the Oder, and to eradicate the last German bridgeheads on the Oder's east bank, but now in early April two army groups – the First Belorussian Front and the First Ukrainian Front – stood poised to begin the final attack on the German capital. Further south the Second and Third Ukrainian Fronts had entered the Ostmark (former Austria annexed to the Reich) and were closing in on Vienna.

On the Italian front, the Allied 15th Army Group, comprising the US Fifth Army and British Eighth Army, after a winter pause of nearly four months, was about to unleash its Spring offensive, aiming to capture Bologna, cross the Po river, and drive for the Alps in order to seal off the Germans' main escape route from Italy – the Brenner Pass.

And in the West, the Allied armies under General Dwight D. Eisenhower – a mighty force of nearly four and a half million men – had crossed the Rhine river on a broad front and were now streaming across Germany in multiple drives against rapidly diminishing German resistance. In the south, the US 6th Army Group, consisting of the US Seventh and French First Armies, had broken out of its bridgehead and was making good progress, pushing the remnants of two German armies before it. The Americans were moving east and had reached Würzburg and the French were driving south along the east bank of the Rhine towards Karlsruhe.

In the centre of the front, the US 12th Army Group, fielding from north to south the US Ninth, First and Third Armies, had just on April 1 completed encirclement of the Ruhr industrial area – the centre of German armaments production – and its main force was now racing towards the Elbe river, hoping to split Germany in two by linking up with the Soviets advancing from the east. On the army group's left flank, the US Ninth Army was approaching the city of Hannover, a city that would fall within a day, and after that would continue towards Magdeburg. In the centre, the US First Army was driving around the Harz Mountains and thrusting directly east for Leipzig. And on the right wing, the US Third Army was streaming into Thuringia and aiming for Chemnitz and Dresden.

Planning for Operation 'Amherst' was begun on March 29, 1945 and the operation was launched on April 7. This map shows the situation on the western front in the first week of April.

And in the north, the British 21st Army Group under Field-Marshal Bernard Montgomery was advancing to its final objectives. Its right wing, the British Second Army, was pushing across the north-German plain and driving for Bremen, Hamburg and the Baltic ports. Its left wing, the Canadian First Army, after crossing the Rhine at Rees in Germany, had made a hard left turn and had re-entered the Netherlands, but now on the north side of the Rhine.

The Canadian Army's intention in this final phase was to have its left wing, the Canadian I Corps under Lieutenant-General Charles Foulkes, capture Arnhem and then move to seal off the German forces holding out in the western part of Holland, while its right wing, the Canadian II Corps under Lieutenant-General Guy Simonds, lashed out to clear the north-eastern part of the country and reach the North Sea. For this final offensive, Simonds could muster four divisions, the Canadian 2nd and 3rd Infantry and 4th Armoured Divisions and, in a later phase, the Polish 1st Armoured Division.

It was in this situation that on March 28 a plan was proposed to help the Canadian advance to the North Sea by means of an airborne operation. Available in the United Kingdom, fully trained, up to strength and eager to go, were two French parachute battalions belonging to the elite Special Air Service (SAS). They were the 2ème Régiment de Chasseurs Parachutistes (known to the British as 4th SAS) and the 3ème Régiment de Chasseurs Parachutistes (3rd SAS). The idea was to drop these French parachutists behind the German lines with mission to seize important bridges and play havoc with the Germans and thus facilitate and speed up the Canadian advance. Thus it was that Operation 'Amherst' was born.

THE FRENCH SAS

BY LATE MARCH 1945 the Special Air Service Brigade was concentrated in Britain. Having started out as a small-party raiding and sabotage unit in the Western Desert in 1941, the SAS had expanded considerably in four years of war and by now had consolidated into a full brigade comprising five battalions: the 1st and 2nd SAS (both British), the 3rd and 4th SAS (both French) and the 5th (Belgian) SAS.

The two French battalions were better known by their French names, the 2ème Régiment de Chasseurs Parachutistes (2ème RCP) and the 3ème Régiment de Chasseurs Parachutistes (3ème RCP). The 2ème RCP (4th SAS) had its origins in the two French SAS Squadrons that had fought in Libya and Tunisia in North Africa in 1942-43. Brought to Britain in late 1942 and early 1943, and merged with Free French volunteers that had reached England

The 2ème Régiment de Chasseurs Parachutistes (4th SAS) marching down the Champs-Elysées on November 11, 1944. (ECPAD)

in other ways, it became the 4ème Bataillon d'Infanterie de l'Air, renamed the 2ème RCP in March 1944. The 3ème RCP (3rd SAS), originally the 3ème Bataillon d'Infanterie de l'Air, had been raised in French North Africa in June 1943, enlisting volunteers from Algeria, Corsica, Syria and Lebanon; evaders from France, and men from Général Henri Giraud's army. Brought to Britain in October 1943, it was re-designated the 3ème RCP and together with its sister regiment joined the SAS Brigade.

The 2ème RCP jumped into Brittany on D-Day, dropping sabotage parties and forming the ill-fated SAS bases 'Samwest' and 'Dingson', and continued its battles there in company with the Maquis until early August. In mid-July, the 3ème RCP joined the fray, dropping a squadron near Brest and then sending missions to the Loire and Limousin regions. August-September saw the 2ème RCP, now completely Jeep-borne, fighting in the eastern Loire region, while the 3ème RCP did the same in central eastern France, fighting in Burgundy and Franche-Comté, its Jeep squadron penetrating deep into enemy territory to reinforce the various parties. These actions continued well into October. To make up for the losses suffered in all these operations – 112 killed and 230 wounded – the battalions absorbed and trained numerous new recruits, most of them young volunteers from Maquis resistance groups in liberated territory.

The 2ème RCP then again saw action during the Battle of the Bulge, patrolling and securing the left flank of the US VIII Corps on the southern side of the German penetration from December 24. By February 19, 1945, both battalions were back in Britain and billeted in army camps, the 2ème RCP at Orwell Park, and the 3ème RCP at Rendlesham Hall, both outside Ipswich in Suffolk.

On March 21, the SAS Brigade received a new commander, Brigadier Mike Calvert taking over from Brigadier Roderick McLeod. A veteran commander of Chindit missions in Burma, Calvert was well versed in commando-like operations behind enemy lines.

By this time of the war, with the British Army suffering from an increasing shortage of infantry, higher headquarters were wondering why such a large and well-trained formation was being left unemployed in Britain. At the same time, commanders and troops in the SAS Brigade were chafing to see combat before war's end. This combined into a situation where many were looking for ways to use the SAS troops before it was too late.

OPERATION 'AMHERST'

ON THE MORNING OF March 28, Brigadier David Belchem, Chief of Operations and Planning at Field-Marshal Bernard Montgomery's 21st Army Group Headquarters, asked Calvert to come and see him with regard to the possibility of employing SAS troops in conjunction with the First Canadian Army in Holland. Calvert told him what resources were available

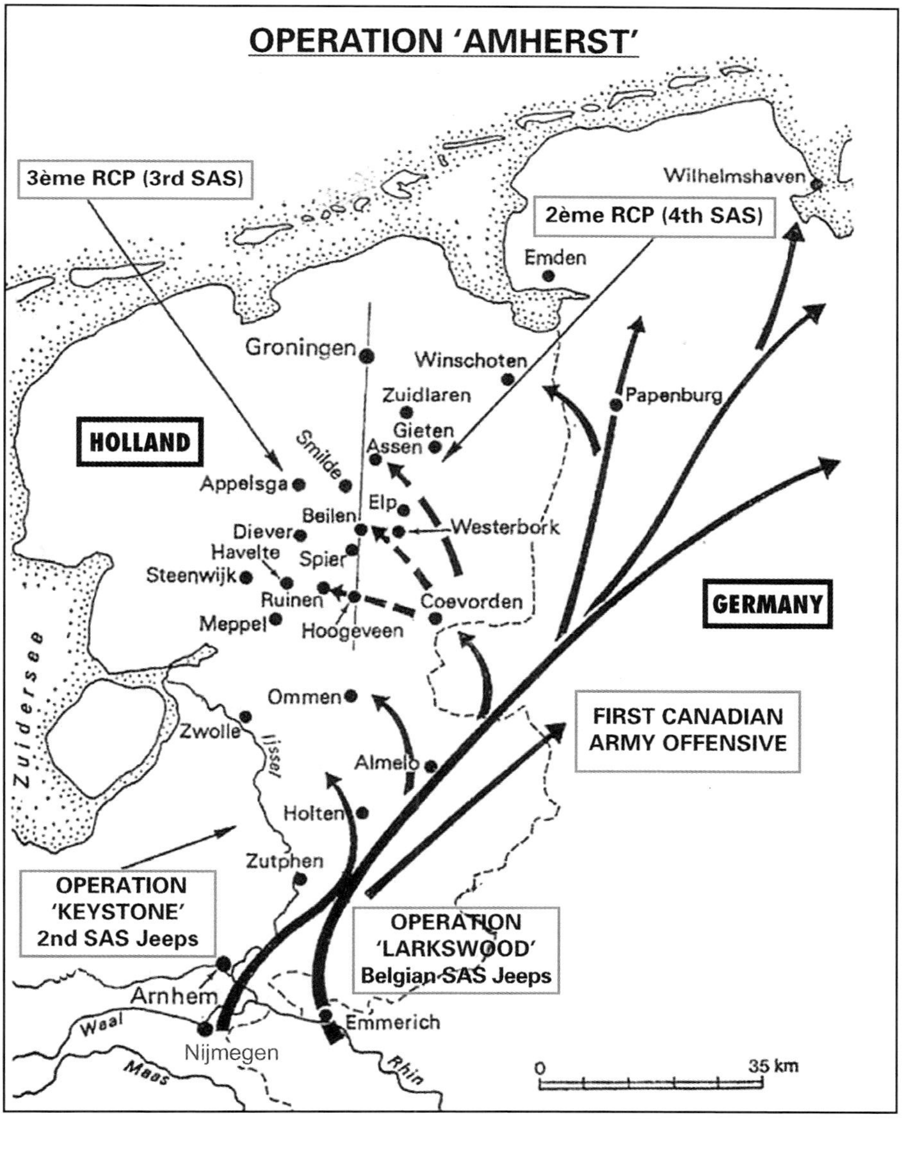

Operation 'Amherst' involved the dropping of two French SAS parachute battalions in north-eastern Holland in order to facilitate the advance of the First Canadian Army to the North Sea. Simultaneously with it, two other SAS operations were planned on either side: 'Larkswood' would deploy the 5th (Belgian) SAS in a ground role with Jeep teams operating ahead of the Canadian 4th Armoured Division, and 'Keystone' would see the 2nd (British) SAS operate west of the IJssel river to assist the Canadian advance towards western Holland.

Major-General Richard Gale, commander of the British I Airborne Corps, of which the SAS Brigade formed part, addressing the troops of the 2ème RCP at their base camp in Orwell Park near Ipswich in Suffolk.

Gale inspecting the 3ème Squadron of the 3ème RCP at Orwell Park during the same visit. Behind him are Lieutenant-Colonel Jacques de Bollardière, commander of the 3ème RCP (left) and Brigadier Mike Calvert, commander of the SAS Brigade (right). The 3ème RCP had its base camp at Rendlesham Park but had come to Orwell Park for the inspection.

and Belchem rang this through to Brigadier Churchill Mann, the Chief-of-Staff of the First Canadian Army. The following day, March 29, Calvert flew to First Canadian Army Headquarters, which was then at Grave near Nijmegen in the Netherlands, to confer with Mann. The latter described the army's intentions and suggested an area in north-east Holland where the two French battalions could operate to great advantage.

On March 24, the First Canadian Army had begun crossing the Rhine at Rees in Germany. It had then wheeled sharply left, re-entering Holland from the east, and its Canadian II Corps now stood poised with two infantry and one armoured division in a cramped area along the line Emmerich–Doetinchem, ready to begin its northward advance through north-east Holland towards the North Sea. It was here that the Canadians saw a role for the SAS.

Calvert explained to Mann that SAS troops were trained and organised to operate in small parties of about one officer and ten to 15 men, either parachute-dropped or Jeep-carried, and could best be used dispersed over a wide area to cause utmost confusion and prevent a retreating enemy from forming a new line. He stressed that they did not have the heavy arms to fight pitched battles and could therefore not be expected to take and hold any objectives against an organised attack. He expounded that in the present circumstances the parachutists should be overrun, i.e. relieved by the advancing ground forces, within 72 hours after being dropped.

The following day, March 30, at a meeting chaired by Colonel Ted Beament, the Canadian Army's Chief Operations Officer, and attended by Calvert, Lieutenant-Colonel W. B. G. Reynolds, the army's GSO1 (Air), and Lieutenant-Colonel Maurice De Rome, the Special Forces representative at Canadian Army HQ (responsible for SOE and 'Jedburgh' operations), an agreement in principle was reached to use SAS troops in the Canadian sector.

That same afternoon Calvert wrote out an appreciation on the use of SAS troops for General Henry Crerar, the Canadian Army Commander, in which he explained the technicalities of SAS parachute and Jeep operations and considered the pros and cons of using SAS troops in the area envisaged. In a meeting later that same day, General Crerar accepted Calvert's suggestions and gave his approval for three SAS operations. On the army's right flank, the 5th (Belgian) SAS would be deployed in a ground role with Jeep teams operating ahead of and in conjunction with the Canadian 4th Armoured Division, soon to be replaced by the 1st Polish Armoured Division (Operation 'Larkswood'). In the centre, the two French parachute battalions would be dropped to facilitate the northward advance of the Canadian 2nd Infantry Division to the North Sea ('Amherst'); and on the left, 2nd (British) SAS would operate west of the IJssel river to assist the Canadian advance towards western Holland ('Keystone').

The general plan for Operation 'Amherst' was for the 2ème and 3ème RCPs to be dropped in the triangle formed by the towns of Groningen, Coevorden and Zwolle about 48 hours in advance of the leading ground

Major Pierre Puech-Samson, commander of the 2ème RCP.

Lieutenant-Colonel Jacques de Bollardière, commander of the 3ème RCP.

On April 4, three days before the launch of 'Amherst', the two French SAS battalions were moved to a concentration area close to their departure airfields. Here men of the 2ème RCP stand waiting at Orwell Park for transport that will take them to their new destination.

From 1945 to 2016. On May 26, veterans of the 7th Armoured Division (The Desert Rats) attended a commemoration at the memorial in Orwell Park School to remember the men of the 22nd Armoured Brigade, including the 5th Royal Horse Artillery, who were camped in the grounds before moving to Normandy. The French SAS were stationed there from February 1945 onwards. (Adrian Brown)

elements of Canadian II Corps with the following tasks: (1) to cause the maximum confusion throughout the area and thus prevent the enemy from taking up any fixed positions; (2) to try and prevent demolition of bridges by removing the demolition charges in order to hasten the advance of Allied ground forces; (3) to try and preserve Steenwijk (Havelte) airfield for the use of the Royal Air Force; (4) to pass all available information on enemy dispositions back to First Canadian Army and subordinate formations; (5) to provide guides for the advance of the ground forces, and (6) to raise resistance in the area.

By rolling out an airborne carpet in front of the ground forces in order to secure bridges to speed up the advance, 'Amherst' was in effect a kind of miniature version of Operation 'Market-Garden', the Arnhem undertaking of the previous September.

The decision to launch 'Amherst' was delegated to Lieutenant-General Guy Simonds, the commander of the Canadian II Corps. First Canadian Army initially estimated that the earliest this operation would be required would be April 14, which was then two weeks away. (As it turned out, it was launched seven days earlier.)

Having now secured deployment of his brigade, Calvert flew back to his headquarters at Halstead in Essex and gave Colonel Guy Prendergast, his deputy, an outline of the planned mission. The following day, April 1, Calvert visited Air Vice-Marshal James Scarlett-Streatfeild, the commander of No. 38 Group, RAF (which was to provide the troop-carrying aircraft), at his headquarters at Marks Hall in Essex and informed him of the plans. By this time the earliest launching date had already been drawn forward to the night of April 5/6, just four days away.

On April 2, Colonel Prendergast and two SAS staff officers flew to Canadian Army Headquarters and, in two days of meetings with the Army staff and representatives of No. 38 Group, RAF and No. 84 Group, RAF (which was to provide air support and resupply), drew up the detailed plans.

The two French battalions were to be dropped in a triangular area 40

Mushroom Farm (Station 1090) was an army camp near Braintree in Essex that served as the central holding camp for SAS units assembling for operations. Here the SAS men were sealed in to be briefed, issued with weapons and kit, and await the green light for the operation.

The operational plan for 'Amherst' included an air-drop of 18 Jeeps, nine to each battalion, to be delivered to six different drop zones, three Jeeps to each zone (see the table on page 28). The dropping per parachute of heavy loads such as Jeeps or 6-pounder anti-tank guns was still largely experimental in 1944-45. First test drops of Jeeps had shown that its chassis could not possibly take the landing shocks. To rectify this, a sub-frame was fitted under the vehicle and a top frame above, the two connected by rods so that the Jeep was sandwiched between two strong structures, which supported it at many points and held the various heavy units such as engine and axles in relation to each other. Under this sub-frame were fitted crash pans.

All projections on the Jeep were faired off by metal fittings or wire rope-guards so that in the event of somersaulting any rigging line that became wrapped around the load would slip off. To reduce the somersaulting, the Jeep was tilted forward as it fell from the bomb bay of the aircraft; this forced it to somersault against the force of the slipstream, which gave the opposite effect. It also positioned the load at right angles to the parachute rigging lines and produced more-satisfactory results.

kilometres wide at the base and stretching 60 kilometres from south to north. Dividing line between their respective sectors was the north-south Assen to Hoogeveen railway line, with the 2ème RCP assigned the area to the east and the 3ème RCP the one to the west. The parachutists were to drop in sticks of either 15 or 12 men, each stick commanded by one or two officers. Each stick of 15 was to be sub-divided into two self-contained half-sticks for operations. The 12-man sticks were each to comprise three Jeep crews of four men each.

They were to secure a total of 22 objectives: 18 canal and river bridges and four airfields. (This part of Holland, the province of Drenthe, was fragmented by numerous waterways, the main ones being the Hoogeveense Vaart, Beilervaart, Oranjekanaal and Drentse Hoofdvaart canals. In all they featured nearly 150 bridges.) The 2ème RCP was to seize and hold 11 bridges (nine road, two railway); the 3ème RCP was to secure (in order of priority) two airfields at Steenwijk, another one at Eelde (near Groningen), five road and two railway bridges and, lastly, the airfield at Leeuwarden.

It proved difficult to find suitable dropping zones but final plans were agreed on at SAS Brigade HQ on April 4. In all, there were to be 20 drop zones, each of which would be the target of one to three sticks.

Each battalion would land with four wireless transmitting sets with which

The aircraft used was the Halifax bomber, which had a bomb bay large enough to hold two Jeeps. For 'Amherst' each of the 18 aircraft was to hold and drop only one Jeep. In the event, the Jeep drops were cancelled at the very last minute as there was still 10/10th cloud and reception lights could not have been seen.

Initial experiments showed that a cluster of 12 32-foot canopies could be satisfactorily released and this system was used for the first Jeeps dropped in operations (to SAS units in Brittany in June 1944). Later a cluster of four larger parachutes was used.

they could maintain contact with SAS Brigade HQ in England. In addition, every half-stick was issued with a small receiver set, each with a separate code, through which they could receive instructions through the BBC.

The air plan called for the two French battalions to be flown to Holland in one lift of 65 aircraft supplied by No. 38 Group, RAF. The parachutists were to fly in 47 Stirling aircraft, 23 of them carrying the 2ème RCP and 24 the 3ème RCP. Eighteen Halifax aircraft were to parachute-drop 18 armoured Jeeps, nine for each battalion. (A Jeep could be dropped suspended from four large parachutes.)

The parachutists were to depart from three airfields in Essex and Suffolk: Rivenhall, Great Dunmow and Shepherds Grove. From Rivenhall, 16 Stirlings of Nos. 295 and 570 Squadrons would carry 16 sticks of the 2ème RCP to six different drop zones. From Great Dunmow, 16 Stirlings of Nos. 190 and 620 Squadrons would carry 16 sticks – seven of the 2ème RCP and nine of the 3ème RCP – to eight different drop zones. The remainder of the 3ème RCP would depart from Shepherds Grove in 15 Stirlings of Nos. 196 and 299 Squadrons, which would aim for six different drop zones. In addition to dropping a stick, each Stirling was also to drop four containers, two carrying food and two carrying a Bren gun and mixed ammunition. Time interval between aircraft dropping on the same DZ was set at ten minutes.

The 18 Jeeps were to be carried by 18 Halifaxes of Nos. 296 and 297 Squadrons departing from Earls Colne and aiming for six different drop zones (each of them also the target of at least one parachute stick), the plan being to drop three Jeeps on each DZ. The vehicles were to be dropped about one hour after the parachute sticks had jumped, the latter having set up beacon lights to guide them in. Unfortunately, the French SAS paras had

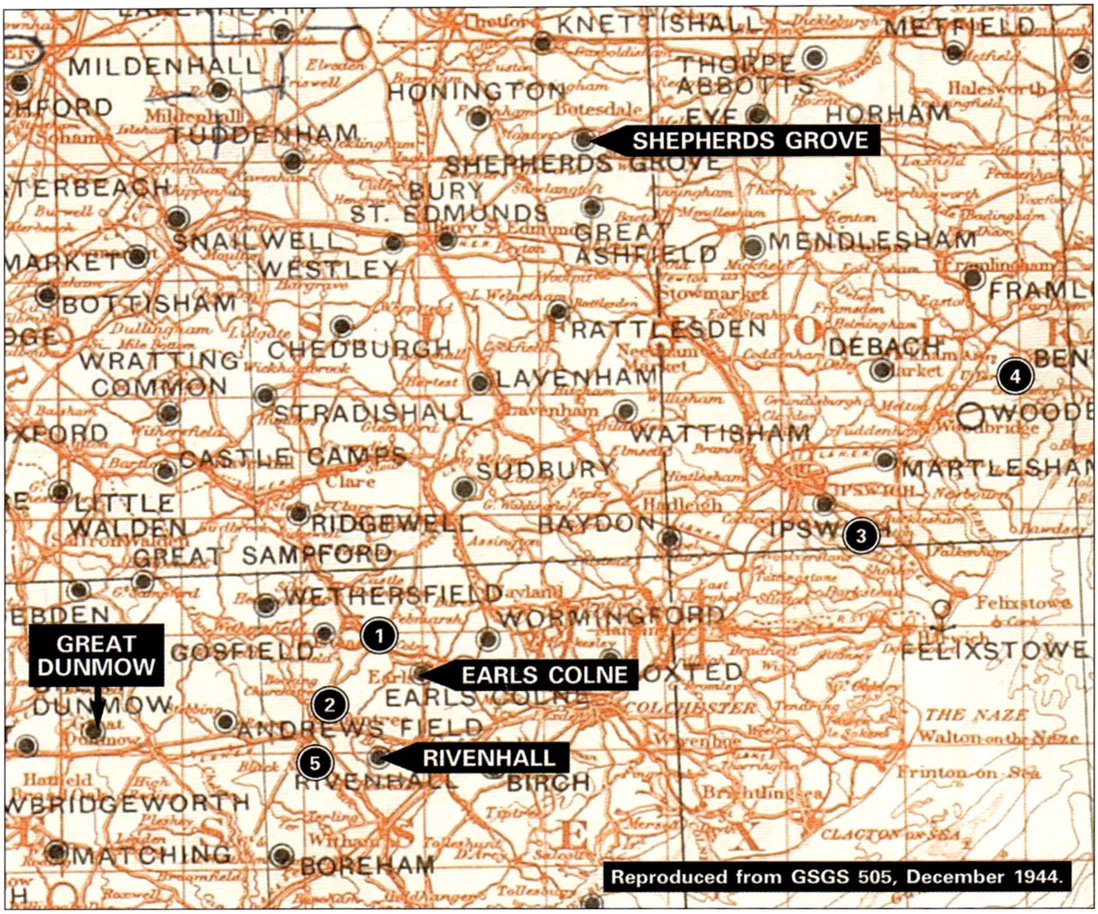

The parachute missions were to depart from four airfields, the 2ème RCP from Rivenhall and Great Dunmow, the 3ème RCP from Great Dunmow and Shepherds Grove, and the 18 regimental Jeeps (to be parachute-dropped) from Earls Colne. Other locations indicated are [1] SAS Brigade HQ at Halstead, [2] No. 38 Group HQ at Marks Hall, [3] Orwell Park, [4] Rendlesham Park and [5] Mushroom Farm.

never been trained to drop from the same aircraft that carried the Jeeps, so by necessity their crews (four to a Jeep) had to fly in Stirlings with the rest of the troops and jump separate from their vehicles.

The aircraft would fly in over friendly territory, their route first crossing the Channel to Brussels in Belgium and then turning on a north-easterly course to Enschede in the Netherlands and then north to the various drop zones. No. 38 Group had made clear that they feared friendly anti-aircraft fire more than enemy Flak or night-fighters, so First Canadian Army ordered a complete anti-aircraft silence over the whole 21st Army Group area for the night of the drop. Finding the correct dropping zones would be done by means of Gee, the radar navigation system which pinpointed a target by means of crossing two radio beams. To deceive the enemy into thinking that a much-larger airborne operation was underway, the deception plan called for 143 simulators (dummy parachutists with ammunition set to detonate when touching ground) to be dropped from the Stirlings. Also, prior to the drop, medium bombers of No. 2 Group, RAF were to attack selected targets to create the impression of a larger attack area (this part of the scheme was later scratched).

As the troops were to be relieved within 72 hours, resupply air drops by No. 38 Group were considered unnecessary. Instead, Typhoon fighter-bombers of No. 84 Group would be on call to drop supplies in containers.

Canadian Army intelligence estimated enemy strength in the 'Amherst' area at 12,000, of which 9,000 were coast defence troops and 3,000 reinforcements and recruits of the 1. Fallschirm-Armee. Canadian intelligence had lost track of the 6. Fallschirmjäger-Division, which was moving west to take up the line of the Twente Canal between Zutphen and Hengelo and units of this division could perhaps be expected in the 'Amherst' area, together with numerous rear-area troops.

As regards the role of the Dutch resistance in the operation, their strength was not believed to be very thick on the ground due to the fact that the open and flat terrain in that part of Holland offered little concealment and did not lend itself well to organising Maquis-like activities, so the planners did not reckon with any large-scale support from Dutch interior forces. Lieutenant-Colonel De Rome certainly wanted to raise what armed resistance groups were active in the area but both he and Calvert were reluctant to give them an early warning lest it jeopardise the security of the operation. It was therefore agreed that a code-message mobilising the resistance – 'De boot is omgeslagen' (The boat has capsized) – would only be broadcast via Radio Orange (the Dutch service on the BCC) on D+1.

On completion of the operation, all parachutists were to rendezvous at the airfield at Steenwijk-Havelte.

First Canadian Army issued its operational order for 'Amherst' early on April 5. By then the earliest target date was set for the night of April 6/7. If the operation was on, SAS Main HQ was to be alerted by 7 a.m. preceding the night of the drop and No. 38 Group by noon of that day.

Having completed the outline plans, Prendergast and his staff flew back to England. The following day, April 4, he briefed the French battalion commanders, Major Pierre Puech-Samson of the 2ème RCP and Lieutenant-Colonel Jacques de Bollardière of the 3ème RCP, telling them to make their preliminary plans forthwith. That same day, the two French SAS battalions were moved into a concentration area at Mushroom Farm, an army camp near Braintree in Essex, for equipping and briefing, working out the details of each stick, and packing the Jeeps in parachute crates. Although the two battalions had a combined strength of about 900, quite a few of the new recruits had not yet completed parachute training and in the end only some 700 were selected to go on the operation (339 of the 2ème RCP and 357 of the 3ème). The French paras were very eager to go. The morning before the drop, six French privates were in hospital in Paris with injuries or sickness. Within six hours of having heard that an operation was to take place, they landed at Earls Colne, just in time to report for duty.

That evening, Brigadier Calvert visited the French, delivering a speech in which he said:

> 'You are about to proceed on a very important operation, which I hope will make up for the disappointments you have suffered in the cancelation of other operations. Your job is to cause the maximum confusion in the enemy lines, to save some bridges from destruction in order to increase the speed of our advance and by your example to raise the resistance movement in the area. Think over all the training you have done and the operations you have carried out, so that you lose no opportunity to put your experience into practice in what might be the last battle of the European war.'

As Calvert recalled:

> 'At the end of my briefing, I decided that a little humour might relieve the strain so I took rather longer than necessary over my description of the type of country they would find. "It's all pretty flat and very largely farmland. I'm told there is also plenty of game to be had, such as hares and pheasants . . ." They stared for a moment, then broke out into cheers and roars of laughter. They were a gay crowd and their morale was terrific.'

The following day, April 5, Calvert flew to Canadian Army Headquarters and set up a small Tactical HQ SAS Troops there, from which he planned to oversee and control the operation. To keep up with developments, he had arranged that any messages from the parachutists received at SAS Main HQ in England would be passed on to him via a Phantom radio link or by teleprinter. Also, Phantom sets at Canadian Army could intercept the wireless traffic between the paratroops and SAS Main.

The following day, April 6, Calvert visited General Simonds to arrange the timing of the operation. Calvert felt somewhat hurried as earlier that day Coevorden, at the south-east corner of the 'Amherst' area, was taken by the Canadian 4th Armoured Division and several of the proposed dropping zones were already overrun, too near Allied lines to be effective, or already within the Allied bomb-line. That evening, General Simonds ordered the drop to take place on the following night, that of April 7/8, weather permitting.

A message to that effect immediately went out to SAS Main HQ and to No. 38 Group. With little more than 24 hours to go, there was a hurried re-organisation of the plans, with last-minute changes in drop zones, hasty briefings of pilots and sticks on their changed missions, and re-arrangements for the radar control. The final drop zones were not fixed until 11 a.m. on April 7, just nine and a half hours before the first aircraft were to take off. As it finally turned out, six of the originally selected 25 drop zones (Nos. 1, 2, 5, 7, 9 and 14) were cancelled and 19 zones actually used, ten by the 2ème RCP and nine by the 3ème RCP.

'AMHERST' IS LAUNCHED

ON THE AFTERNOON OF April 7, the two French battalions were driven to their departure airfields. It was here that some of the deficiencies of the troops' parachute training became evident. Many of the men had to be shown how to correctly put on their parachute harness, and hurried rehearsals were necessary to show everybody how to attach and release the leg-bags. Many of the Stirling aircrews stepped in, helping the men to arrange kit and parachutes. Owing to the last-minute changes in dropping zones, adjustments had to be made to ensure that the right sticks were on the right aircraft, with each of them knowing where they were now going to

In the afternoon of April 7, the troops were taken to the airfields. After kitting up, many sticks had a group photo taken. This is stick No. 11 of the 2ème RCP commanded by Aspirant Marcel Edmé, pictured at Great Dunmow. (ECPAD)

Captain Albert Fay, the British liaison officer attached to the 2ème RCP (left), and Capitaine Gualberto Larralde, second-in-command of the battalion's HQ Squadron and leader of stick No. 21 (right), awaiting plane embarkation at Great Dunmow.

drop. The language problem did not ease the situation and there was much rushing-about and confusion.

A late arrival at Great Dunmow was a four-man 'Jedburgh' team' (code-name 'Dicing'), sent out by Special Forces Headquarters and tasked with organising the Dutch resistance in the area. Led by British Major Robert Harcourt and further comprising Dutch Captains Carel Ruys van Dugteren and Arie Bestebreurtje and British radio operator Sergeant Claude Somers, they were assigned to fly as part of stick No. 21 of the 2ème RCP.

At this late hour, an unexpected hitch occurred. With weather forecasts predicting low clouds and thick fog over the dropping zones, the No. 38 Group commander, Air Vice-Marshal Scarlett-Streatfeild, got in touch with Major-General Richard Gale, the commander of I British Airborne Corps (to which the SAS Brigade was subordinated) at his headquarters at Rickmansworth in Hertfordshire, to discuss whether the operation should be on. He stated that with such bad visibility he could not guarantee extreme accuracy in the drops. Such accuracy was particularly needed for the dropping of the Jeeps, since their crews would be waiting for them on the DZs. Under the circumstances, Scarlett-Streatfeild said he did not think the dropping of Jeeps of any value, as they would almost certainly go astray. Gale agreed and at 1900 hours decided to cancel the Jeep drop. It was a very last-minute decision and with great consequences for the operation for much of the SAS's planned tactics were based on the mobility provided by the Jeeps. It was taken so late that the French commanders and Jeep team leaders only learned of it while already emplaned or even after take-off, and some of them never learned of it at all. At least one Jeep team leader, Lieutenant Denys Cochin of the 2ème RCP, spent a whole night at his agreed dropping zone, ready with beacon lights, waiting in vain for his vehicles to be dropped. (After the operation, Brigadier Calvert was extremely angry with Prendergast, his deputy, for having conceded to the Jeeps being cancelled without any protest.)

Take-off on the three airfields began at 2030 hours and was completed one hour later. All 47 aircraft took off, except one. A Stirling of No. 620 Squadron at Great Dunmow had engine trouble and was unable to take off. The 15 parachutists, stick No. 23 of the 2ème RCP under Aspirant Pierre Lagèze (one of the Jeep teams), transferred to another aircraft but by the time they were ready it was too late to go. (The stick would drop the following night).

Sous-Lieutenant Jack Quillet, also of Larralde's stick. They were to jump on Drop Zone 8 and there to await the arrival of three of the battalion's Jeeps – which never came.

Another stick composed of Jeep crews of the 2ème RCP, this one No. 23 commanded by Aspirant Pierre Lagèze, also pictured at Great Dunmow. As it was, their aircraft was the only one that failed to take off that night, and the stick was dropped the following night, April 8/9.

Sixteen miles east of Great Dunmow, other men were preparing at RAF Rivenhall. Posing here are (L-R) Soldat Marcel Mougne, Caporal Fernand Bégue, Caporal Victor Estève and Sergeant Jean Reilhac, all four from Lieutenant Jean Appriou's stick No. 3 of the 2ème RCP.

Sous-Lieutenant Henry Corta's stick No. 10 of the 2ème RCP posing at their Stirling aircraft at RAF Rivenhall. Posing with the 15 parachutists, on either side, is the six-man aircraft crew from No. 295 Squadron.

Forty-five miles to the north, at RAF Shepherds Grove, stick No. 20 of the 3ème RCP had their picture taken before putting on their parachutes. This stick was commanded by Capitaine Gilbert Paumier.

The other 46 aircraft had an uneventful flight to Holland and all of them dropped their sticks between 2330 and 0045 hours. Released with them were 185 containers, plus 30 more for the Dutch resistance. In addition, prior to reaching the DZs and afterwards, 14 of the Stirlings dropped a total of 143 dummy parachutists with simulators. There was no anti-aircraft fire anywhere and all Stirlings returned to base safely. The only trouble encountered was that some of the dummy parachutists had caught on the tail of the aircraft and the blank charges had gone off immediately, the detonating ordnance causing the aircrews to think that they were being chased by enemy fighters all the way back to England!

In all, 691 men jumped. Only one man, Aspirant Pierre Roux of stick No. 15 of the 3ème RCP, was unable to jump, his parachute having opened inside the aircraft, and he returned to England aboard the Stirling. (He would arrive overland with the Jeeps on April 10). In another aircraft – the one carrying stick No. 20 of the 3ème RCP under Capitaine Gilbert Paumier – the dispatcher, British Sergeant Andre Philips, himself jumped after his stick, armed only with a Colt revolver, and he fought with the French paras throughout the battle.

As always, there were casualties in the landings. Two men, Lieutenant Louis de Sablet and Sergeant Yago Ragnacci, both of the 3ème RCP, fell into water and drowned. At least ten men broke a leg or seriously sprained an ankle on hitting ground. One officer, Capitaine Pierre Sicaud,

Map from the RAF official report on Operation 'Amherst' showing the flight routes from the UK airfields to the drop zones in north-eastern Holland. The aircraft – flying not in formation but singly, as was custom for British airborne operations – first flew south to a turning point above Tonbridge in Kent, crossed the coast above Dungennes, made landfall over Cap Gris Nez in France, then flew over Allied-held territory until they reached their respective Initial Points (final turning points) between Goch and Enschede, where they turned north to their respective drop zones. The return trip was made via a northern route over the North Sea. (UK National Archives)

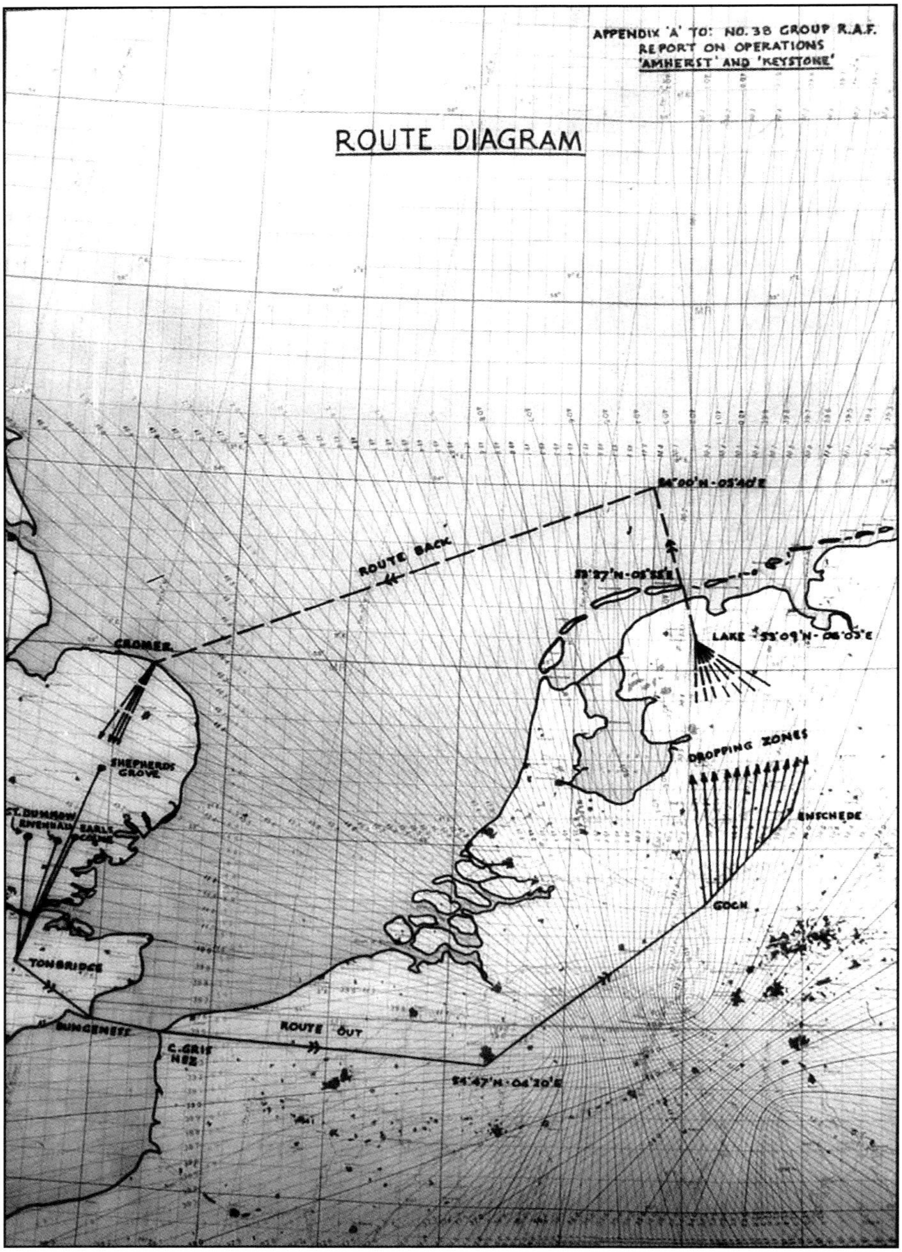

Right: **Map from Brigadier Mike Calvert's official report on Operation 'Amherst' showing the 19 drop zones used and indicating with thin arrowed lines where the sticks destined for these zones actually landed. The numbers at the end of the arrows are not the stick numbers as used by the two regiments (1 to 23 for the 2ème RCP and 1 to 24 for the 3ème RCP) but the aircraft chalk numbers, which were different and ran from 1 to 65. They add up to 65 because they include the 18 aircraft assigned to drop the Jeeps – a part of the mission that was cancelled at the last minute. For some unexplained reason, stick No. 13 of the 3ème RCP (chalk 51) is missing from the map – it landed near No. 10 (chalk 54) close to DZ 16. Drop zone 12 was used again (re-numbered 26) on D+1 to drop stick No. 23 of the 2ème RCP (chalk 7), which had failed to take off on the first night.** (UK National Archives)

ASSEN
Gieten
Gasselte
Borger
Appelsga
Smilde
Beilen
Westerbork
Spier
Elp
Schoonlo
Diever
Achterdijk
Meppen
COEVORDEN
12 26
11
21
13
22
4
10
16
23
8
15
24
3
6
20
25
19
18
17

PARACHUTE MISSIONS FOR OPERATION 'AMHERST'

Aircraft Chalk No.	*Airfield*	*RAF Squadron*	*DZ*	*Stick No.*	*Unit or Load*	*Stick Commander*	*Remarks*
					2ème Régiment de Chasseurs Parachutistes		
1	Rivenhall	295	21	18	HQ Sqd/2 RCP	Lasserre	
2	Rivenhall	570	21	19	HQ Sqd/2 RCP	Bourrel	
3	Rivenhall	295	22	16	HQ Sqd/2 RCP	Gramond	
4	Rivenhall	570	22	17	HQ Sqd/2 RCP	Berr	
5	Great Dunmow	620	3	13	3 Sqd/2 RCP	Leblond	
6	Great Dunmow	620	3	14	3 Sqd/2 RCP	Nicol	
7	Great Dunmow	620	3	23	Jeep crews/2 RCP	Lagèze	jumped on DZ 26 on D+1
8	Earls Colne	296	3		Jeep		drop cancelled
9	Earls Colne	296	3		Jeep		drop cancelled
10	Earls Colne	296	3		Jeep		drop cancelled
11	Rivenhall	295	4	5	1 Sqd/2 RCP	Simon	
12	Rivenhall	570	4	6	1 Sqd/2 RCP	Stéphan	
13	Rivenhall	570	4	20	HQ Sqd/2 RCP	Varnier	
14	Rivenhall	295	10	3	1 Sqd/2 RCP	Appriou	
15	Rivenhall	570	10	4	1 Sqd/2 RCP	Sriber	
16	Rivenhall	570	10	2	1 Sqd/2 RCP	Forgeat	
17	Great Dunmow	620	6	8	2 Sqd/2 RCP	De Camaret	
18	Great Dunmow	620	6	11	2 Sqd/2 RCP	Edmé	
19	Rivenhall	295	24	7	2 Sqd/2 RCP	Legrand	
20	Rivenhall	295	24	10	2 Sqd/2 RCP	Corta	
21	Rivenhall	570	24	9	2 Sqd/2 RCP	Gabaudan	
22	Rivenhall	295	25	1	HQ Sqd/2 RCP	Puech-Samson	
23	Rivenhall	295	25	15	3 Sqd/2 RCP	Taylor	
24	Rivenhall	570	25	12	3 Sqd/2 RCP	Betbèze	
25	Great Dunmow	620	8	21	Jeep crews/2 RCP	Larralde	
26	Earls Colne	296	8		Jeep		drop cancelled
27	Earls Colne	296	8		Jeep		drop cancelled
28	Earls Colne	296	8		Jeep		drop cancelled
29	Great Dunmow	190	23	22	Jeep crews/2 RCP	Cochin	
30	Earls Colne	296	23		Jeep		drop cancelled
31	Earls Colne	296	23		Jeep		drop cancelled
32	Earls Colne	296	23		Jeep		drop cancelled
					3ème Régiment de Chasseurs Parachutistes		
33	Great Dunmow	190	11	1	1 Sqd/3 RCP	Rouan	
34	Great Dunmow	190	11	2	1 Sqd/3 RCP	Ferchaud	
35	Earls Colne	297	11		Jeep		drop cancelled
36	Earls Colne	297	11		Jeep		drop cancelled
37	Earls Colne	297	11		Jeep		drop cancelled
38	Great Dunmow	190	12	3	1 Sqd/3 RCP	Valayer	
39	Great Dunmow	190	12	4	1 Sqd/3 RCP	Poli-Marchetti	
40	Earls Colne	297	12		Jeep		drop cancelled
41	Earls Colne	297	12		Jeep		drop cancelled
42	Earls Colne	297	12		Jeep		drop cancelled
43	Great Dunmow	190	13	5	1 Sqd/3 RCP	De Sablet	
44	Great Dunmow	190	13	6	1 Sqd/3 RCP	Boiteux	
45	Great Dunmow	190	13	7	1 Sqd/3 RCP	Boulon	
46	Earls Colne	297	13		Jeep		drop cancelled
47	Earls Colne	297	13		Jeep		drop cancelled
48	Earls Colne	297	13		Jeep		drop cancelled
49	Great Dunmow	620	15	8	2 Sqd/3 RCP	Tupet-Thomé	
50	Great Dunmow	620	15	9	2 Sqd/3 RCP	Hubler	
51	Shepherds Grove	299	15	13	2 Sqd/3 RCP	Vidoni	
52	Shepherds Grove	299	16	11	2 Sqd/3 RCP	Collery	
53	Shepherds Grove	299	16	12	2 Sqd/3 RCP	Duno	
54	Shepherds Grove	299	16	10	2 Sqd/3 RCP	Sicaud	
55	Shepherds Grove	299	17	14	3 Sqd/3 RCP	Baratin	
56	Shepherds Grove	299	17	15	3 Sqd/3 RCP	Bouffartigue	
57	Shepherds Grove	299	17	16	3 Sqd/3 RCP	Lagallarde	
58	Shepherds Grove	196	18	17	3 Sqd/3 RCP	Gayard	
59	Shepherds Grove	196	18	18	3 Sqd/3 RCP	Marchal	
60	Shepherds Grove	196	19	19	HQ Sqd/3 RCP	De Bollardière	
61	Shepherds Grove	196	19	20	HQ Sqd/3 RCP	Paumier	
62	Shepherds Grove	196	19	21	HQ Sqd/3 RCP	Dreyfus	
63	Shepherds Grove	196	20	22	HQ Sqd/3 RCP	Vallières	
64	Shepherds Grove	196	20	23	HQ Sqd/3 RCP	Grumbach	
65	Shepherds Grove	196	20	24	HQ Sqd/3 RCP	Lecomte	

Table showing the details of the 65 aircraft deployed in 'Amherst': their chalk numbers, departure airfields, RAF squadron to which they belonged, assigned drop zone, stick number, SAS unit (or Jeep load) aboard the aircraft and stick commander. The final column shows that only one stick, No. 23 of the 2ème RCP, was unable to take-off on D-Day and jumped a day later (and on a different drop zone as originally planned) and that all of the 18 Jeep-dropping missions were cancelled.

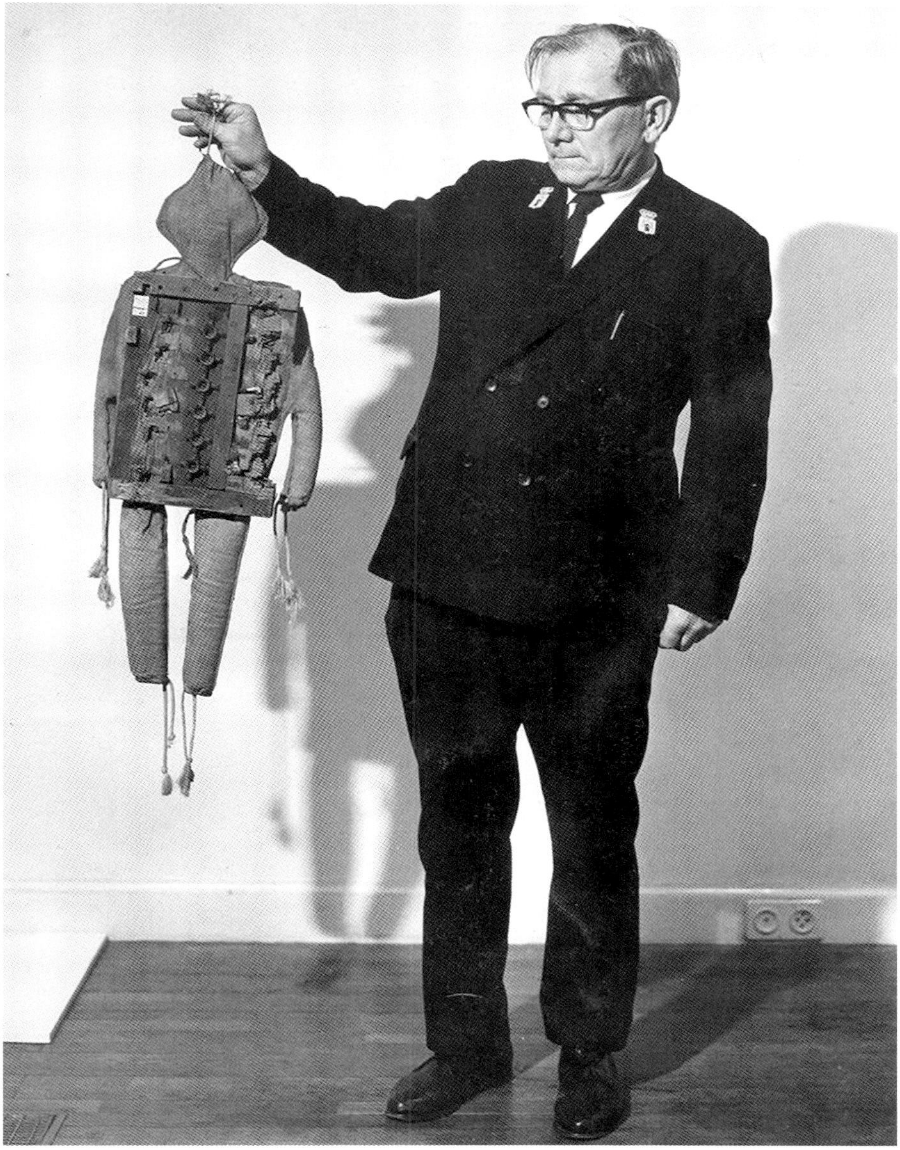

In addition to the 700 parachutists, the Stirlings dropped a total of 143 dummy parachutists. Fitted out with simulators that could imitate either rifle, machine-gun or mortar fire, they were supposed to confuse the enemy into thinking that a larger force had landed over a wider area. The dummy shown here was actually dropped in 'Amherst' and later recovered.

commander of the 2ème Squadron of the 3ème RCP (stick No. 10), dropped into a pine forest and was blinded for three days.

The drop did not accomplish great accuracy, the majority of the 46 sticks landing wide off the mark. Most came down between two and ten kilometres from their assigned dropping zones, with several landing even further away, and one stick as far as 45 kilometres from its DZ. Only six of the sticks landed precisely on the correct zone.

The mis-drops were caused by an unforeseen problem with the Gee navigation radar. Gee worked best when the two beams sent out by its stations intersected at a 90-degree hook, giving a clear indication when the receiving aircraft was directly above the target. However, the mobile Gee radar stations with First Canadian Army had had insufficient time to change to geographically better-suited positions and the result was that

Map showing all the towns and villages mentioned in our story. The Assen to Hoogeveen railway line (marked bold) was the boundary between the 2ème RCP and 3ème RCP, the former dropping east and the latter west of it.

the angle of cut of the radar beams was so narrow, only about 16 degrees, that accuracy was considerably impaired.

In addition to coming down in the wrong place, sticks also landed widely dispersed. With 10/10th cloud at 2,000 feet, the paras were dropped at between 1,500 and 2,000 feet altitude, which meant that their parachute descent lasted nearly two minutes. Coupled with the strong wind (13.5 knots or 25 kmh) this caused the paras to drift even further from their DZ and land far away from each other.

Due to the mis-drops, many sticks spent their first hours trying to discover where they were. Some knocked at farm doors, others stopped Dutch civilians out on a stroll (it was a Sunday) or questioned civilians they happened to bump into. In general, the Dutch proved of great assistance, providing guides, information and food, and taking care of wounded. On the other hand, this part of Holland contained a relatively large proportion of collaborationists, members of the Nationaal-Socialistische Beweging (NSB, Dutch Nazi party) and other Nazi sympathisers, and there were quite a few cases where Dutchmen betrayed the presence or hiding location of French paras to the German authorities.

To increase their problems, the paras found that the maps they had been issued with were not very good. Aerial photos of their DZs and targets had been taken on the afternoon of April 5 but there had not been time to issue each stick with prints. However, this was not the only thing that hasty planning and last-minute changes had caused to go wrong. For example, on recovering their containers after landing, several sticks found that the Bren guns packed in them were still in their factory grease and had to be cleaned before they could be taken into use. Other sticks failed to recover all their containers (This later led to the persistent misconception that many of the Stirlings had been loaded with only two instead of the prescribed four containers).

Another thing that went amiss was rear-link communications. Each half-stick had been given its own receiver and unique code to receive instructions through the BBC. However, broadcasting time was limited to only four hours a day and it proved impossible to pass messages for each of the 46 sticks in that time; there was also no general code in which one could communicate with all sticks rapidly. The result was that many sticks were left in the dark as to what higher headquarters expected of them once the operation got under way.

Despite the problems encountered, the French paras everywhere went into action with great audacity and zeal. All through the area, ambushes were laid on roads, German vehicles and horse transport were shot up, bridges were scouted out and, if found intact, de-mined and held for as long as could be safely done. With sticks coming down all over the area, each one had its own individual adventures and encounters.

The Germans reacted immediately and violently, instituting large search and destroy operations, attacking known French positions and, in

Two of the parachutists landed in water and drowned. Both are still buried in the Netherlands. *Left:* **The grave of Lieutenant Louis de Sablet d'Estières, leader of stick No. 5 of the 3ème RCP, in the municipal cemetery on Witterweg in Bovensmilde.** *Right:* **The grave of Sergeant Yago Ragnacci from stick No. 21 of the same regiment in the General Cemetery on Torenlaan in Beilen.** (Karel Margry)

several instances, executing captured parachutists under Hitler's infamous Kommando-Befehl. They also took reprisal measures against Dutch civilians suspected of having helped the French, arresting people and carrying out executions.

THE 2ème RCP

ONE OF THE EARLIEST and most-spectacular French actions was also one of the most costly. Stick No. 12 of the 2ème RCP, led by Capitaine Alexis Betbèze, commander of the battalion's 3ème Squadron, came down near the small village of Garminge, well south-west of its planned DZ. After assembling his men, Betbèze heard from Mr Kuiper, a school teacher in the nearby village of Witteveen, that a German general had his headquarters in the village of Westerbork, six kilometres to the north-west.

This was Generalmajor Karl Böttger, the commander of Feld-kommandantur 674, the Wehrmacht district in north-eastern Holland. Originally stationed in the city of Groningen, the day before Böttger had been ordered to set up a defensive line along the Hoogeveense Vaart with four companies of Feldgendarmerie and another along the Oranjekanaal further south with two newly-arrived Luftwaffe battalions.

Looking for a bivouac in nearby Witteveen wood, Betbèze stumbled upon Major Puech-Samson, his battalion commander, and his stick of Squadron de Commandement (HQ Squadron) personnel. He too had heard about the German general in Westerbork from H. P. Th. van Lohuizen, the director of the magnetic observatory in Witteveen. Together, Puech-Samson and Betbèze decided to attack the German command post, which was in the Café Slomp in the centre of the village. However, before they set out, two Dutch policemen appeared. One of them, Opperwachtmeester Derk-Jan Stoel, told the Frenchmen (with Van Lohuizen acting as his interpreter) that he lived next-door to the Café Slomp and gave valuable information on the situation in the village, enabling Puech-Samson and Betbèze to draw up a plan of attack. Stoel returned to Westerbork, promising he would return at 1 p.m. to guide the French in. When he showed up again, he brought with him an Allied agent. This was Sergeant Wim van der Veer, a Dutch Commando who had been dropped

A sizable group of the 2ème RCP under the battalion commander, Major Pierre Puech-Samson, assembled in a wood near the small village of Witteveen, making it their base of operations for the duration of 'Amherst'. This photo of Puech-Samson was taken in their forest hide-out. (ECPAD)

into Holland the previous October as an SAS weapons instructor (SAS team 'Portia'). As it happened, Van der Veer had for a time stayed in hiding in Stoel's house, he knew Westerbork well, and it was decided that he instead of Stoel would guide Betbèze and his 18 men to the target.

At 3 p.m. on April 8, the SAS party entered the village, approaching the Café Slomp from the rear. However, the Germans spotted them and opened fire. Wim van der Veer recalled:

> 'As we advanced toward our objective, the people were happy and calm. They couldn't believe their eyes and were utterly surprised. And then we encountered W. I knew him, as I knew all the Landwachters. I saw him ride past on his bicycle. He wasn't in uniform that day. I was walking next to Betbèze and I said to him: "That man is a traitor." The French immediately arrested him, and I searched his pockets and retrieved a pistol and a dagger.
>
> 'Why didn't we kill him? It's hard to believe; the French wanted to do it immediately, but I said, "Stop, he's unarmed and defenceless, we'll drag him before a court". And he went with us as a prisoner.
>
> 'The point, consisting of a sergeant and two soldiers, was 50 metres ahead of the rest of the group. After half an hour, we reached the first houses in the village, a school, and two farmhouses. Between the school and the farmhouses was an excavation, a kind of embankment, which could serve as a start line. We managed to advance to this start line unnoticed by the Germans. A few residents did see us, but at my beckoning, they didn't give any sign. Between the start line and the houses where the Germans were lay a meadow and a field that we had to cross during the assault. That was the weakest and most risky point. How far would we get before the Germans noticed us?
>
> 'From my cover, I had a good view of the garden of Café Slomp – the German headquarters – and next to it, the gardens of Derk-Jan Stoel and Doctor Boezeman. It was strangely quiet, too quiet, actually. Suddenly, a German soldier cycled right past us. He spotted us, got startled, and speeded off, apparently to warn the others. Lieutenant Le Bobinnec took aim and fired, and the soldier lurched across the road like a drunken man and collapsed on the side of the road. At that moment, everything went out of control. Captain Betbèze got up and shouted a few orders in French, after which the entire group, firing from the hip, charged across the meadow and field, straight toward Café Slomp and the command post.'

The Frenchmen went into the assault, one section charging at the café and another crossing the village street to attack it from the front. Generalmajor Böttger, in long leather coat and brandishing a machine-pistol, emerged from a front door. Hit by a bullet, he fell gravely wounded (the French were convinced he was dead, but he survived). Two other German officers, Oberstleutnant Max Busse and Rittmeister Wilhelm Janssen, who also came

Having heard that a German general had his command post in the nearby village of Westerbork, Puech-Samson sent Capitaine Alexis Betbèze's stick and half of his own stick to attack it. The headquarters was in the Café Slomp in the centre of the village. The attack developed into a short, sharp battle in which Generalmajor Karl Böttger, was grievously wounded and some 20 other Germans killed or wounded, but which cost the SAS three men killed and four officers wounded, two of them captured by the Germans. (Wybo Boersma Collection)

The former Café Slomp, today the Hotel-Restaurant De Westerburcht, still stands at No. 7 Hoofdstraat. (Karel Margry)

out, were killed. An intense firefight raged for over an hour, hand-grenades being thrown by both sides and bullets smashing windows all around, until finally the Germans gained the upper hand and the French were forced to withdraw.

The two German officers killed in the attack, Oberstleutnant Max Busse and Rittmeister Wilhelm Janssen, today lie in the German military cemetery at Ysselsteyn in the southern Netherlands. (Johan van Doorn)

Capitaine Betbèze recalled the attack:

> 'Everyone rushed forward, and I cannot understand how, with our load, our equipment, our number and our exhaustion, we managed to pass the numerous barbed-wire fences. I found myself in front of the hotel-café, at grips with the Feldgendarmes; Adjutant Jean Bouard, who backed up the right, had to infiltrate to the general's house. I noticed a first burst of automatic fire coming from a window, the clatter of glass and the dust of the broken window. The burst was intended for me and Soldat Paul Gautray, who was on my left. I looked at Gautray, he still was on his feet; Gautray looked back, I was also still standing. The enemy gunman must have been very nervous to have missed us. Caporal Robert Bonjean's Bren gun jammed after the first blasts. Caporal René Marché, Sergeant-Chef Djamil Jacir and some other men had taken cover behind the single trunk of an apple tree about ten metres from the hotel to answer the fire. I gave the order to turn left and quickly take cover behind a house, which would protect us from the enemy fire. One of the men – probably Marché – shouted: "We'll go down like rabbits trying to cross that fence". I shouted back: "Better to get shot running than to get shot lying still. Follow me!" Those who followed me were saved. Marché and Sergeant Jacir remained in place to fire at the hotel windows and the attic dormer windows. Bonjean, rather than circle around the building by jumping

Capitaine Betbèze's stick posing for a group photo a day or two later – now only 11 strong having lost four of its members (two men killed and two men captured) in the Westerbork action. Betbèze is kneeling right. Note the light-coloured scarfs worn by several of the men, actually yellow recognition panels issued to each man as means of identification to friendly fighter-bombers.

> the barbed-wire fence, ran forward into the main street; carrying his unusable Bren gun.
>
> 'He stopped in the middle of the road, turned toward the hotel-café and knelt. Had he seen an enemy sniper at one of the windows? He took out his Colt, pointed towards the hotel, as if to point out the shooter's position and then aimed. Before he could fire a shot, he was hit. With a groan he fell in the street, his head covered in blood. I immediately tried to rescue him but when I moved out into the street a bullet ricocheted off the road between my feet and a splinter hit me in my right calf; I quickly jumped back into cover.'

Sous-Lieutenant Alain Le Bobinnec led the attack on the right:

> 'I approached the hotel-café and entered through the kitchen. The Germans spotted us and opened fire. An officer left the house, a sub-machine gun in his hand. He was wearing the insignia of a general. A burst through the kitchen window, and he fell to the ground. At that moment, Adjutant Bouard also opened fire. We stepped over the general's body; he was badly hit, blood pouring from his abdomen, and he didn't move.
>
> 'A German lieutenant left the hotel through the front and only saw us from three metres away. A bullet in his back, and he fell.

Prior to the attack, Puech-Samson had received detailed information on the German headquarters from a Dutch policeman, Opperwachtmeester Derk-Jan Stoel, who lived two doors away from the Café Slomp and had come cycling up to the Witteveen woods with a colleague to pass on information that allowed the French to draw up a plan of attack. The assault group was then guided to the target by another Dutchman, Willem van der Veer, who was actually an Allied secret operative. A sergeant in Dutch Troop of No. 10 (Inter-Allied) Commando, Van der Veer had jumped into Holland six months earlier as part of an SAS mission to the Dutch resistance and had been acting as a weapons instructor ever since. Always in hiding, he had stayed for a while at Stoel's house, so he knew Westerbork well. After the action, the two men were photographed together: (L-R) Opperwachtmeester Stoel, his wife Joke, Sergeant van der Veer. (Wybo Boersma Collection)

The picture was reputedly taken outside the Stoel's house at No. 11 Hoofdstraat. However, although it looks similar, it is clearly not the same house. (Karel Margry)

The war memorial outside Westerbork's town hall includes a plaque ***(right)*** **honouring the SAS parachutists and their motto 'Du ciel la liberté' (Freedom comes from the sky). Sculpted by Charles Hammes and dedicated in 1949, the plaque was originally in the façade of the town hall but when a new war memorial was created in 2004 it was added to that one.**
(Karel Margry)

'A major also spotted us, but he didn't have time to re-enter the hotel-café; a bullet hit him in the chest. Shots were fired from the upstairs windows. The front door was barricaded. It seemed too late to retrieve any documents. The Germans had had time to burn them.

'A grenade landed on the roof, and Bouard crept along the building to a position below the upper windows so as to throw in hand-grenades. Behind us in the village we heard shots. We destroyed the radio and were then ordered to withdraw.

'Pulling out, I met Capitaine Betbèze, who had attacked the hotel-café from the front. Two of his machine guns had malfunctioned. One gunner had been killed, a second wounded. As I approached the captain, I was also hit. He took me in his arms and carried me out of the combat zone. Then he too was wounded. Four hours later, I was still alive but I couldn't stay there. I dragged myself to a cellar where I met two Dutchmen. They gave me something to drink and stopped the bleeding. I stayed in the cellar until 10 a.m. the next morning. Caporal Robert Bonjean, who was with me, died that night. Then the Germans came and I was taken prisoner.'

Van der Veer had watched the attack from behind the village school:

> 'I stayed there because I was in civilian clothes and not authorised to carry a weapon. I could only watch and hope that everything would turn out well. Suddenly I said to myself: "Damn, where has W. gone?" He had run off as soon as the attack began. I was so fascinated by what I saw that I completely forgot about him. I did, however, have his pistol.'
>
> 'It was a fierce battle that lasted at least an hour. At one point, we received a message indicating that an SS force was approaching. I don't know how that message got through. Someone came to deliver it to me. After that, the French retreated toward Witteveen. I stayed in the school building for a while and then outside to see what would happen after the attack on the command post. Then I saw a Frenchman [Caporal Jean-François Cornet] lying behind a pile of straw, behind the doctor's house. He was wounded. The Germans attacked him from both sides simultaneously and threw grenades to finish him off.'

The Germans had lost ten men killed and about 20 wounded, but the SAS had suffered too. Nearly half of Betbèze's force had become casualties: three men killed – Caporals Robert Bonjean, Jean-François Cognet and René Marché – and four men wounded: Betbèze himself, Sous-Lieutenants Edouard Lorang (the battalion Intelligence Officer) and Alain Le Bobinnec, and Adjutant Jean Bouard. The latter two were found by the Germans and taken prisoner.

A chaotic and tense situation reigned in the village after the attack, as ambulances evacuated the many German wounded and excited Germans held and questioned local inhabitants suspected of having assisted the attackers. Seven of them were detained at the café for several hours but eventually all were released.

Just four kilometres east of Westerbork, stick No. 8 of Lieutenant Michel de Camaret, the commander of the 2ème Squadron, had landed in the fields between the Oranjekanaal and the Schoonloo woods to the north. Before dawn, De Camaret and his men had set up a base at the farm of the Pol family on the north bank of the canal. At the lieutenant's request, farmer Matthijs Pol and his 15-year-old son Hendrik-Jan went out with their horse and cart to bring in Caporal-Chef Jules Brasse who had sprained his ankle in the jump. At 7 a.m. several SAS men joined De Camaret at the farm: one half of stick No. 15, led by Aspirant Maurice Richard, which had got separated from the stick's other half (and from their stick leader, Sous-Lieutenant Georges Taylor); plus Sergeants Georges Mahé and Pierre Pacifici and Caporal-Chef Antoine Treis, who had been unable to find their own stick, No. 22. With those reinforcements, De Camaret now had 26 men to fight with.

Just a kilometre to the south-east was a bridge across the canal, leading to the village of Orvelte. Halfway towards it, there was also a canal lock with foot bridges across the lock gates. Just beyond the locks, on this side of the canal, stood a large building, the flax-mill of H. F. Reijntjes. Both the Orvelte

Four kilometres north-east of Westerbork, stick No. 8 of the 2ème RCP, led by Lieutenant Michel de Camaret, set up in the barn of the farm of the Pol family on the north bank of the Oranjekanaal near Orvelte. Here farmer Matthijs Pol and other family members pose for a snapshot with the French paras at the barn. (Wybo Boersma Collection)

bridge and the locks were valuable objectives so shortly after dawn, shielded by a thin early-morning mist, De Camaret led his men towards them.

However, during the night, a force of 50 Luftwaffe soldiers had taken up position in another farm, that of Arend Enting located just beyond the flax-mill, and eight of them were guarding the canal lock, armed with rifles and Panzerfäuste. A fierce firefight erupted, two of the Germans being killed and two of the Frenchmen – Aspirant Richard and Sergeant Mahé – being wounded. The guard detail was overwhelmed but the noise of combat had alerted the other Germans in the Enting farm and they reacted immediately. As De Camaret's men prepared to dash across the open backyard of the flax-mill a volley of fire rang out, killing Caporal-Chef Treis with a bullet through the throat.

Soon the French position became untenable and De Camaret ordered a withdrawal. Taking their two wounded and six prisoners with them, they withdrew to the Pol farm, continuing on into the Schoonloo woods, both for better cover and to safeguard the Dutch family from reprisals.

German troops – a mixture of SS, Organisation Todt and Landwachters (Dutch Nazi militia) – soon engulfed the farm, searching for enemy soldiers. They discovered Caporal-Chef Brasse, injured in the jump, and took him

Further down along the canal stood a flax-mill and close by was a canal lock with footbridges, guarded by a German detachment. In the early morning fog, De Camaret attacked this position, hoping to capture the sluice bridges and maybe the drawbridge at Orvelte, a kilometre further on. (Wybo Boersma Collection)

The flax-mill still stands along the canal. De Camaret's men nearly overwhelmed the bridge detail but then came under fire from other Germans and were forced to pull back.

A memorial cross today commemorates the single SAS soldier killed in the action, Caporal-Chef Antoine Treis. The plaque and cross were originally mounted on the rear wall of the mill, at the spot where Treis fell, but in 2011 were moved to the front of the building to make them more prominent. (Karel Margry)

Three days after the action, on April 11, armoured Jeeps – the Jeep platoon of the 2ème RCP under Capitaine Robert Moulié with two vehicles and B Company of the 5th (Belgian) SAS with ten vehicles – reached the Oranjekanaal from the south (they had begun operations from Coevorden that day). Together with De Camaret's men and Dutch civilians, they improvised a bridge over the locks, enabling the Jeeps to cross over to the north bank where they relieved several sticks of the 2ème RCP that were still fighting in the Schoonloo woods. (Wybo Boersma Collection)

The small house on the south bank helps to pinpoint the exact spot where the Jeeps crossed. (Karel Margry)

prisoner. They threatened to hang the Pol family but farmer Matthijs Pol convincingly played innocent and the family got away unharmed.

Later that day, at 3 p.m., another firefight broke out at yet another farm along the canal, that of farmer Berend Mulder located about a kilometre north of the Pol farm, when a German patrol bumped into the half-stick under Sous-Lieutenant Taylor. The latter was killed, hit by two bullets in the stomach; the other five Frenchmen got away.

Two of the Belgian Jeeps (distinguishable from the French Jeeps by the chalked names on the windshield) were pictured at the Pol farm. (Wybo Boersma Collection)

Below left: **The farmhouse stood unchanged until 2007 but was then pulled down to make way for a new house, built by the new farm owner Geert Willems** ***(below right)*****, which however looks remarkably similar and still makes for a good match. The barn where the parachutists were photographed has also been replaced with a modern version.** (Wybo Boersma/Karel Margry)

De Camaret's men posing near the locks with members of the Pol family and inhabitants of the other farms along the Oranjekanaal. (Wybo Boersma Collection)

Both farms seen in the background have made way for modern buildings, the one on the left (No. 42) in identical style but the one on the right (No. 43) in an altogether different architecture. (Karel Margry)

Stick No. 5 of the 2ème RCP under Sous-Lieutenant André Simon came down near the village of Westdorp. As they emerged from a farm where they had asked for information, they became involved in a fire encounter with a group of Germans who had been warned of their presence by another farmer. Caught in an open field with only straw bales for cover, three of the Frenchmen were killed and four wounded, three of which were taken prisoner. In April 2016, on the 71st anniversary of the action, this small memorial was unveiled, across the road from the farm at No. 9 Schoonloërstraat, to commemorate the three men killed: Caporal-Chef Albert Le Saux, Caporal René Péron and Soldat Serge Levasseur. (Karel Margry)

On a tree on the north bank of the Oranjekanaal at the village of Wezuperbrug is a small plaque commemorating three other French SAS troopers: Sergeant-Chef Robert Le Gras, Sergeant Gabriel Judet and Sergeant Aimé Le Berrigaud. Members of stick No. 20 of the 2ème RCP under Lieutenant Andre Varnier, they were killed in a regular battle with German troops in the Ellertsveld woods north of the village on April 9. The fight over, their bodies were roped to a vehicle and dragged behind it to Wezuperbrug where they were dumped alongside the canal. When they were found, this led to a persistent story, widely accepted for decades, that they had been executed under the regulations of Hitler's Kommando-Befehl. The plaque was put up by an SAS veteran, former Sergeant Gilbert Hentschké of the same stick, in 2007 about one kilometre east of the Wezuperbrug canal bridge, but unfortunately not quite at the correct spot where the bodies had been found. (Karel Margry)

Ten kilometres north-east of Westerbork, stick No. 5, under Sous-Lieutenant André Simon, landed outside the small village of Westdorp, and shortly after assembly, their presence betrayed by a Dutch farmer, became involved in a firefight with a group of German Fallschirmjäger. Three men were killed (Caporal-Chef Albert Le Saux, Caporal René Péron and Soldat Serge Levasseur,) and three others (Caporal Charles Besnard and Soldats Jean-Pierre Usséglio and Jean Delasalle) wounded and captured. The rest of the stick, including two more wounded, Caporal Georges Allin and Soldat Charles Dupuis, escaped into the Borger woods. Usséglio described the unequal fight:

> 'Immediately after landing, we quickly regrouped, thanks to the lieutenant's flashlight signals. At dawn, Lieutenant Simon and Aspirant Albert Bornhauser go to a farm, no doubt to determine our location. They swiftly come back with a German prisoner, who is immediately interrogated. That done, they both return to the same farm.
>
> 'Then we see a group of Germans walking along the road and approaching the farm. We open fire, and they dash to some ditches, where they have better cover than us who, hiding in the open field, only have straw heaps.
>
> 'A fierce firefight ensues, in which everyone participates (except Levasseur, who is guarding the prisoner). The well-positioned Péron uses his Bren gun to perfection. Sergeant Pierre Matern is superb. The Germans move as if on a training exercise. One of their men takes off on a bicycle, probably to fetch reinforcements. We plan to break off the fight but are hesitant to do so because Simon and Bornhauser haven't returned yet. One of us, whose name I don't remember, says, "I'm leaving" and quickly takes off toward the woods. He may be a wimp, but he's realistic. At that moment, we should have done the same.
>
> 'Levasseur, still hampered by his duty to guard the prisoner, sits behind his straw heap, muttering to himself. The prisoner, who has seen the Germans advancing in a fan formation, understands that the fight is taking a turn in his favour. Levasseur wants to execute him. I yell at him not to make that mistake.
>
> 'The stick begins to break off the fight, and at the same moment I'm hit by three bullets: in my right shoulder, right hand and right thigh. With great courage, Caporal Georges Allin drags me to the straw heap where Péron is positioned. At that very moment, he's hit, killed instantly. Matern insists that I surrender. According to him, that's the only way to survive and avoid being killed. I call Charles Dupuis, my best comrade. He takes a few steps toward me. Convinced I'm going to be shot, I tell him, "Remember me to my family." Shortly after, I hear that Levasseur and Le Saux are dead.
>
> 'I continue firing at the Germans 20 meters away, to provide cover for Delassale and Besnard, who are crawling through the field without

> much hope of a happy ending. The Germans, moving around the straw heaps, come roaring toward us. Delassale, Besnard and I are captured. Delassale mutters, "For us, the war is over."

The remnants of stick No. 5 eventually managed to join up with a stick from the battalion's HQ Squadron. This was stick No. 20 under Lieutenant André Varnier which had come down about a kilometre north of them. On the second day, April 9, this group came under severe pressure from German search parties, and had to hastily move position. Three members of Varnier's stick – Sergeant-Chef Robert Le Gras and Sergeants Gabriel Judet and Aimé Le Berrigaud – were killed. Their corpses were later found to show wounds from automatic weapons fired at close range, which led to the persistent story that they too had been executed on the spot under the Kommando-Befehl.

Just a few kilometres north of where Simon and Varnier saw action, four sticks had come down in or near the Boswachterij Gieten, a tract of wood

Four sticks of the 2ème RCP dropped near to each other and assembled in the Gieten woods, forming a force of 60 men and setting up a base from which to lay ambushes on the roads in the area. Two of the men, Aspirant Victor Stéphan, the assistant doctor, and Soldat Jean Troller, both of Lieutenant Jean Appriou's stick No. 3, carried a camera into battle, making this group one of the most-photographed of the whole of 'Amherst'. Posing for this group shot is stick No. 7 led by Lieutenant Michel Legrand (who is himself not in the picture). (ECPAD CTT-14-325)

located within the triangle of the towns of Rolde, Gieten and Borger. They were sticks Nos. 3 and 6 of the 1er Squadron, led by Lieutenant Jean Appriou and Sous-Lieutenant Henri Stéphan respectively; stick No. 7 of the 2ème Squadron under Lieutenant Michel Legrand, and stick No. 16 of Capitaine Pierre Gramond, the commander of HQ Squadron. Quickly making contact with each other, and now some 60 men strong, they set up a base in the Gieten wood from which they could lay ambushes on three main roads passing it: the Assen–Rolde–Gieten road on the north side, the Gieten–Gasselte–Borger road on the east side and the Rolde–Borger road on the west side.

However, en route to lay a first ambush on the Rolde to Gieten road on the night of April 8/9, one of the scouts, Sergeant Guy Lesné of Legrand's stick, was killed at the Huis Heidehof estate and nothing came of this first attempt.

On the second day, April 9, the group attacked the headquarters of the Nationalsozialistische Kraftfahr-Korps (National Socialist Motor Corps, NSKK) located in the rectory at Gasselte, the village just east of their forest hide-out. (Karel Margry)

On the second day, April 9, a patrol reported the presence of a German force in the village of Gasselte, just east of their base in the woods. One detachment, stationed in the rectory of the village church, was in fact the headquarters controlling the units of the Nationalsozialistische Kraftfahr-Korps (National Socialist Motor Corps, NSKK) stationed in occupied Holland. Commanded by a German officer, Obersturmführer Klaus, it consisted mostly of Dutch Nazi collaborators. The French decided to raid the enemy HQ, drawing up a plan for a daylight attack from three sides to start at noon.

Emerging from the wood and advancing through the gardens, the various groups, some 40 men in all, cautiously approached the rectory. However, as they began going around the house they were spotted by the NSKK men who opened fire with rifles and a machine gun, wounding Sergeant Georges Briand and killing Caporal Fernand Bégue. At Appriou's order, two of his men, Caporals Marcel Urbain and Louis Goudivèze, charged across open ground and threw high-explosive and smoke grenades through the front windows, after which the rest of the SAS group closed in, firing their weapons and throwing more grenades. Soon the enemy garrison came out, hands in the air and surrendering. Four of the NSKK had been killed, three wounded and ten captured. The attack was a complete success. Taking their

The assault force comprised three of the four sticks in the group, making up a force of about 40 men. On their way to the target, the men prepared for action at the barn of forest keeper R. Pronk. (ECPAD CTT-14-326)

Pronk's forester's house and barn stood on the edge of the Gieten woods, just inside the trees on the north side of what is today Bosweg. Both buildings have since been pulled down but Willem van Hemmen, who as a seven-year-old heard the gunfire of the fight at the rectory and who today lives on Bosweg, pointed out to us where they stood. (Karel Margry)

POWs, a staff car that stood parked in front of the building, and the body of Caporal Bégue with them, the paras withdrew back into the woods.

Lieutenant Appriou left a good account of the attack:

> 'It was relatively easy to approach the built-up area; woods and undergrowth extended almost to the entrance of the village, providing ideal camouflage. With Lieutenant Legrand's group and my own, we formed a strong unit of 40 parachutists, and soon, upon leaving a wooded area, we saw Gasselte lying ahead of us, clearly silhouetted against a flat plain. Gardens surrounded the village and everything seemed quiet. With binoculars, no activity could be detected, neither by the enemy nor by the villagers. But the straight, flat main street, where the German trucks were neatly parked, was clearly visible.

The attack was a decided success, the NSKK detachment surrendering after a short, sharp fight. This blurred snapshot was taken at the rectory shortly after the end of firing when the men radioed back the outcome of their action to the command post in the wood. (ECPAD)

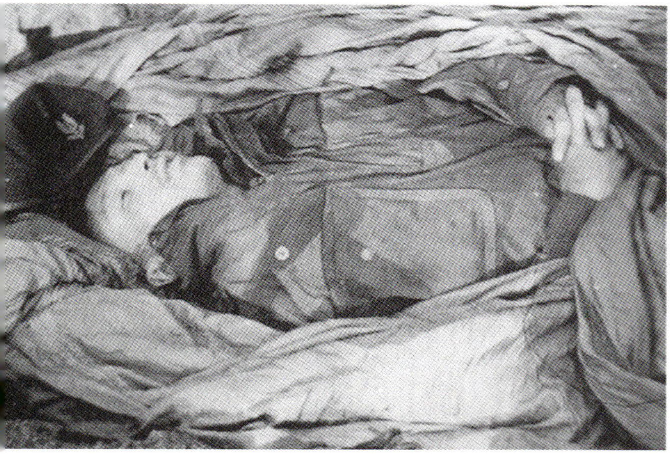

One trooper had been killed in the assault, Caporal Fernand Bégue, hit by a bullet in the throat. (We last saw him posing with his stick members at RAF Rivenhall – see page 24). His body was carried back to the wood camp and buried, wrapped in a parachute. (ECPAD)

Today a memorial in front of the rectory commemorates Bégue's loss. (Karel Margry)

Presumably, there were side streets as well but we couldn't see them clearly from our observation post.

'We draw up the plan of attack, calmly, as if on a training exercise. First, engage the enemy – that will be the mission of Aspirant Albert Bacuez, who will cover the main street with his three machine guns. Then make a flanking movement and encircle the enemy from the other three sides. Lieutenant Legrand will move around on the right and enter the village via one of the side roads. As for me, I have the same mission from the left. Sergeant Louis Le Goff will make a flanking movement with another group at an even greater distance, without seeking combat contact, in order to quickly advance to the

This picture was taken at the site of the action a few days later when the SAS men returned to Gasselte after link-up with the ground army. The rectory building can be seen through the trees. (ECPAD)

They were sitting on the garden fence of the house next-door, No. 1 Dorpsstraat. (Karel Margry)

northern exit of the village and block the road along which any enemy reinforcements might arrive.

'Only one unknown factor remains: how large is the garrison and how heavily armed is it? Not a single member of the Dutch resistance is participating in the operation. But what does that matter? All ideal conditions are never present in the same battle anyway, and today we are almost certain of surprise.

'Bacuez's team occupies a perfect position, covering the entire main street. It has created a perfect field of fire and is guaranteed to destroy anything that appears within it, both infantry and vehicles.

The leaders of the three sticks involved in the attack, pictured as they marched back to their camp (L-R): Lieutenant Jean Appriou, Lieutenant Michel Legrand and Capitaine Pierre Gramond. (ECPAD)

'Thus covered, I begin to advance into the village. We have to go through gardens, over or around fences, and sometimes cut them.

'So far, everything is going well and the enemy isn't reacting in any way. I'm already in the centre, and behind a row of houses an open area appears. In the middle of it stands a building, which I took to be the community building or town hall but was actually the rectory.

'Crossing an open space is always a perilous undertaking; so you have to wait a while because there's almost certainly an enemy there. However, everything remains quiet, which worries me. I order two men to turn back and make a wider encirclement to find out what

The ten prisoners taken at the rectory were taken along into the woods. In front are the two officers captured, Obersturmführer Klaus and Untersturmführer van de Bent, the latter a Dutchman. Most of the personnel in the NSKK detachment were in fact Dutch collaborators. (ECPAD)

the rear of the building looks like. As soon as they begin their circular move they come under fire. This time the enemy has shown themselves; they are indeed in that building.

'Straightaway, all the windows are suddenly opened, with presumably one or more Germans behind each one, their guns pointed in our direction. They're still not firing at us because they're probably waiting for us to rush into that open space, and . . . what an easy target we would be for them then!

'There's no way we're going to attack under these unfavourable circumstances; that would exact a heavy price. So first, those windows must be neutralised, behind which the Germans have much better firing positions, while we ourselves can only take cover behind tree trunks. At a pre-arranged signal, all weapons fire simultaneously at all the window openings, but it's clear that our shots are having virtually no effect.

'But the shooting continues, and I ask Urbain and Goudivèze to prepare for a difficult and dangerous action: while we neutralise the window openings with continuous fire, these two men, under cover of our fire, must advance in leaps and bounds to a blind spot, sneak past the building, with us firing just over their heads, and then throw grenades through the windows. And at that precise moment we will charge forward as fast as possible.

'While all this is being prepared and readied for action, my closest comrade, Sergeant Briand, signals to me that he is wounded. More serious is the rattling I notice to my right: Caporal Bégue, who had exposed himself in order to fire more effectively, is dying: a bullet has ripped open his throat, he dies, choking on his last breaths. It was impossible to help him, so quickly and unexpectedly did the tragedy unfold.

'So, things are getting serious; I already have one killed and one wounded. We resume our fire, more heavily than before, because Goudivèze and Urbain are ready to rush forward. I'm seriously worried about them. Have I not given them an impossible task? But they don't hesitate; they run as fast as they can, yelling as they go. They're already at the front of the building; 12 grenades, including assault grenades, smoke grenades and incendiary grenades, disappear through the windows . . . Now it's our turn to finish the job.

'Forward . . . Ignoring the cover of the trees we run toward the building, pulling the safety pins from our grenades. In seconds the windows are shattered. There's no reaction from inside. Two parachutists walk around the building and throw a Gammon bomb in through the opening in the side wall. Black smoke billows from the windows. The first Germans and Landwachters leave the house, throwing down their weapons and raising their arms. "Comrade!" We search the house and the last Germans emerge. The resistance nest

Lacking a POW cage, the prisoners were roped together using parachute cord. Only the two officers, who had given their word of honour not to escape, were left untied. On the left stands the German staff car that stood in front of the rectory and was used to bring back Caporal Bégue's body. Bégue's field grave can be seen in the background, marked with a white cross. (In 1949, his remains were repatriated to his home town of Antananarivo on the island of Madagascar.) (ECPAD)

is destroyed. We gather the prisoners who will follow us to our patrol base.

'I also have to arrange for Corporal Bégue's transport, and we take him back to the camp in one of the small trucks we captured from the enemy.'

The prisoners tried to fraternise but the French gave them a cold shoulder. Identified here are Soldat Dominique Quénouelle from Legrand's stick (with carbine) and Soldat Emil Soupé looking into the camera. (ECPAD)

Conversing with the prisoners here are (L-R) Lieutenant Appriou, Sergeant Marcel Tricard and Aspirant Guy Merlo. (ECPAD)

Caporals Louis Goudivèze and Marcel Urbain from Appriou's stick. It was their action, charging across open ground in front of the rectory and lobbing grenades through the windows, that had decided the fight at Gasselte. (ECPAD)

Each regiment had been issued with four wireless transmitters and as it happened the radios of both the 1er Squadron and HQ Squadron of the 2ème RCP ended up with this group in the Gieten wood. (L-R) Soldat Troller and Marcel Mougne from Lieutenant Appriou's stick operated the 1er Squadron radio, code-named 'Archiviste 11'. On April 9, Capitaine Gramond used his wireless link to arrange a re-supply drop by Typhoon fighter-bombers, particularly to replenish his dwindling stock of ammunition. (ECPAD)

Caporal Charles Colignon, Caporal-Chef Georges Lalisse (from Gramond's stick) and Sergeant André Renaud operated 'Archiviste 36' of HQ Squadron. Lalisse is turning the handle of the radio's dynamo and Renaud, with headphones, is sending and receiving the Morse messages. (The man on the left has also been named as Soldat Emile Soupé). (ECPAD)

Two brothers meet in combat: Lieutenant Henri Stéphan, leader of stick No. 6, and Aspirant Victor Stéphan, assistant medical officer in stick No. 3. Henri had evaded France in the summer of 1942, had reached Great Britain in May 1943 and had joined the Free French paratroops in July 1943. He had already seen action in Normandy (where he was wounded in combat), in eastern France and in the Ardennes. His brother had joined the SAS from liberated France and was relatively new to the unit, having only gained his parachute wings in December 1944. There were quite a few pairs of brothers in the French SAS, mainly because many replacements were recruited from local Maquis groups. (ECPAD)

Another group photo with (L-R) Caporal-Chef Georges Lalisse, Aspirant Guy Merlo, Sergeant Roger Boutinot and Caporal Charles Colignon (sticks Nos. 3, 7 and 16 of the 2ème RCP). (ECPAD)

Sergeants Georges Briand and Louis Le Goff, also from Appriou's stick, man the Bren gun. Many sticks on landing found that the Bren guns dropped with them in containers were still in their factory grease and had to be cleaned first, which led to precious loss of time on the first night. (ECPAD)

The attack had an aftermath that could have had serious consequences. As soon as the French had left, the locals started plundering the German headquarters. However, two of the NSKK men had escaped capture by hiding in the basement and they witnessed the pillaging from there. When a Luftwaffe company arrived in the late afternoon to re-occupy the village, they reported what they had seen and the German commander, a Hauptmann Willke, thereupon rounded up all 300 men of the village in the Protestant church next to the rectory, threatening to kill them with hand-grenades. The burgomaster, Jan Eldert Tuin, although a member of the NSB (Dutch Nazi party) and appointed by the occupying authorities, bravely pleaded with Hauptmann Willke to refrain from doing so. When the latter then threatened to execute every tenth man in reprisal for the pillaging, the 16 culprits gave themselves up. They were taken to Assen prison but, surprisingly, nothing further happened to them and they were liberated when the Canadians arrived a few days later.

The SAS force in the Gieten wood continued their road ambushes as before. The evening after their raid on Gasselte, two Typhoon fighter-bombers of No. 146 Wing (from airfield B-89 at Mill) dropped four supply containers to replenish their ammunition, food and medical supplies. The following day, April 10, laying an ambush on the Rolde to Gieten road, they

The Protestant Church at Gasselte where the Germans assembled 300 of the village's male inhabitants in order to find out who had pillaged the German headquarters in the rectory after the French raid. The German commander, Luftwaffe Hauptmann Willke, announced deadly reprisals if the culprits did not report in. After a few anxious hours, during which the Nazi burgomaster of Gasselte pleaded passionately for the life of the hostages, the 16 offenders came forward and they were driven off in lorries south to Borgen, where they were locked up in the building of the local ULO secondary school. The next day they were marched back northwards ten kilometres to Gieten where they were put in a cold-storage railway truck in the marshalling-yard, the lack of ventilation nearly suffocating them until one man succeeded in opening a small ventilation grill. The following day, the train drove them to Assen, where they were incarcerated in the local jail. Fortunately for them, liberation came before worse happened to them. (Karel Margry)

shot up a Red Cross ambulance of the Organisation Todt, wounding and capturing a German medical officer. On the fifth day, April 12, the Canadian 8th Reconnaissance Regiment (14th Canadian Hussars), spearhead of the Canadian 2nd Infantry Division, reached Rolde, finally relieving the paras. By then they had amassed a total of 45 POWs which they handed over to the Canadians.

Stick No. 21, commanded by Capitaine Gualberto Larralde and including the four-man 'Jedburgh' team, was one of the 2ème RCP's sticks carrying Jeep crews. Two of them were British, Captain Edward Fay, the British liaison officer with the regiment, and his batman, Private John Corrigan. Destined for Drop Zone 8 south of Assen, the stick landed some four kilometres away to the south-east, near Hooghalen, on the regimental boundary. The stick's second-in-command, Sous-Lieutenant Jack Quillet, recalls:

> 'The light turned green, I yelled "Go!" and dove into the clouds. Swallowed by the night and caught in the blast of the propellers, I heard

The SAS force in the Gieten woods held out until April 12 when they met armoured cars of the 8th Reconnaissance Regiment (14th Canadian Hussars), the vanguard of the Canadian 2nd Infantry Division, at Rolde, west of the woods. Canadian carriers thereupon brought all the SAS troops to Rolde. Gasselte was liberated the next day, April 13, when this picture was taken in Dorpsstraat. First to enter the village, at 4 a.m., was again the 8th Recce Regiment but the Canadians stayed only for a short while, soon moving out again northwards to Gieten. At 8 a.m. they were followed by a column of the 1st Polish Armoured Division, notably Cromwell tanks of No. 2 Squadron of the 10th Mounted Rifles under Captain Jan Salwa, who had been probing north looking for a place to cross the Buinen–Schoonoord Canal.
(Wybo Boersma Collection)

The Bren carrier stood in front of the same house as where the SAS troopers were photographed earlier (see page 52) eating their rations.
(Karel Margry)

a rustle of silk above me; my parachute had opened. I immediately tried to unfasten my leg-bag, but the safety pins were stuck. My nails ripped as I tried to pull that 40-kilo baggage up, thinking about what would happen if I landed with that weight on my feet. A hard thud, my mouth full of water. Suspended in a sitting position, I had landed in one of those countless Dutch canals, which had actually saved me from an even harder blow.

Members of Legrand's stick with Canadian soldiers just prior to being brought from the Gieten woods to Rolde by Canadian carriers. Note that one of them has appropriated and is wearing a German officer's cap. (ECPAD)

Identified on the back of this carrier are (L-R): Soldat Marcel Legendre (left rear), Caporal Louis Goudivèze (with carbine), Aspirant Guy Merlo and Sergeant Louis Le Goff. (ECPAD)

At Rolde the 45 prisoners taken by the four sticks during their various actions and ambushes were handed over to the Canadians. Here they are being marched off to the rear.
(ECPAD CTT-14-329)

The house at No. 15 Hoofdstraat has been altered but is still recognisable.
(Karel Margry)

'Soaking wet, I unfastened my parachute, leg-bag, and rucksack. I headed north, where my comrades were supposed to be, bleating softly, the agreed-upon muster signal. After 100 metres, someone answered and I found Private Pierre Cazenave lying on the ground. "Lieutenant, it's all wrong. I've broken my leg. Don't let me hold you up. Get out of here with the others."

The inhabitants of Rolde were out on the street to celebrate their liberation. Note the two SAS Jeeps in the background. (ECPAD)

The house on the left is in fact the same as the one seen in the previous photo. (Karel Margry)

'I told him to shut up and, supporting him, we headed north. We encountered the uninjured Caporal Jacques Soudain, who went to look for Cazenave's leg-bag. Then we found the also uninjured Caporal Maurice Rutard, and a Scotsman named Corrigan, nicknamed "Paddy", who was Captain Fay's orderly, and finally, Caporal René Lignier, who had sprained his ankle and had walked as far north as he could without encountering anyone. So there were six of us, including two injured, without heavy weapons, without containers, and therefore without ammunition or any additional food.

The Jeeps were those of Jeep Platoon Betbèze of the 2ème RCP, which operated out of Coevorden since April 11 and on the 12th sent patrols to scout out the villages of Borger, Gasselte and Rolde and the town of Assen. This is Jeep M5834315, manned by Aspirant Marcel Edmé and Soldat Etienne Le Chevalier with Soldat Pierre Thonnerieux at the wheel. Standing on the right is Lieutenant Appriou. (ECPAD)

The one behind was M4230250 crewed by Caporal-Chef Jean Contet, Soldat Paul Gautray with Caporal Alain Papazow (AKA as Alain Le Corre, a pseudonym adopted because he was Jewish) at the wheel. (ECPAD)

Today just an unobtrusive parking spot on Hoofdstraat, close to the main road junction in the centre of Rolde.
(Karel Margry)

'I decided to put the two wounded men up in a farmhouse. Paddy and I found one about a kilometre away. The inhabitants were surprised to see who we were and assured us they were patriots. But they refused to shelter our wounded, adding that no one would do so for fear of being punished by the Nazis. We determined our position and discovered that we had been dropped four kilometres from the planned point, near a notorious concentration camp [Westerbork, the transfer camp for Dutch Jews in the Netherlands]. As a result, there was a strong German garrison. The farmers advised us to go to a wood not too far away, where we took our wounded comrades for their safety. We had a terrible time there. We saw the Germans come right up to the woods and, with our few carbines, revolvers and grenades, were unable to do anything against them, as we couldn't break off the fight afterward. One night we tried to head south, but after 500 meters we gave up . . . The terrain was too swampy and there were too many canals.

'After bringing our wounded back to the woods, we decided to contact our own troops, Canadians or others, so that they could take care of them. To do this, we had to cross the Oranjekanaal, which we were north of. When we arrived at the canal, we couldn't find a bridge or a boardwalk. I decided to swim across, but I'd barely reached the near bank when I heard someone say "Wer da?" (Who goes there?) behind me. I turned around, my weapon malfunctioned, and I ran off, straight across the field. Running parallel to the road, I made another attempt 500 meters further on. This time, fire erupted without anyone hailing me. The canal was well guarded.

'After firing shots every now and then for a few minutes and realising the futility of our efforts, we returned to the wood. We were disappointed, but satisfied that we had at least taken action and managed to harass the Germans.'

Quillet's little group remained in the wood until April 12 when they were relieved by Canadian forces.

The Jedburgh team jumping with stick No. 21 had a mixed fate. Major Harcourt was captured on the first day. Captain Bestebreurtje broke his ankle on landing and was out of the battle immediately. However, Captain Ruys van Dugteren and Sergeant Somers, the radio operator, had better luck. They were found by forest-keeper Teun Leever, a member of the Knokploeg Drenthe-Noord, the main armed resistance group in this province, who brought them to a hide-out in the woods near Amen. For the next five days, Ruys van Dugteren radioed through intelligence brought in by the resistance men and women. He also organised an arms drop, a Stirling of No. 38 Group dropping 22 containers to a reception committee of 15 men on a DZ just two kilometres from the Nazi concentration camp at Westerbork on the night of April 10/11. After a hasty weapon instruction by Ruys and Somers, the resistance men used the weapons to harass the Germans until the arrival of the Canadians two days later.

Bestebreurtje described his ill-fated jump:

> 'Finally, at 2245, it's happening. A very poor, slow exit by the French stick, then we quickly follow. It's my first jump from a Stirling, upright through an oblong hole at the rear of the fuselage, and it seems by far the easiest of the many ways I know. After lowering my leg-bag, I find that its cord is around my neck, and with great difficulty, I pull the 60 pounds back up a bit to free myself. Only then can I prepare for the correct landing. On the ground, I see quite a few small lights moving. There's a strong wind and it's foggy. Suddenly, I feel the cord of my leg-bag pulling my legs apart; the leg-bag must have snagged something. Quite unexpectedly, I hit the ground, feel something hard, and an excruciating pain in my right leg. It takes me some effort to get the wind out of my parachute. It also takes an unnecessarily long time to release myself from my jump harness, because I have an unfamiliar strap for my leg-bag attached to it.
>
> 'I try my right foot, and the dreaded thing has happened: my ankle is strained or broken, I can't walk and even crawling, dragging my foot along the ground, is very painful. Realising I must first try to reach our rendezvous, I orient myself briefly with the compass, and begin moving in line with the flight path in the opposite direction. I slowly cover 600 to 800 metres this way, constantly through dense, low bushes, but still don't see anyone from our stick.
>
> 'Knowing that the last four jumped quickly, I decide to crawl back, a little further to the east and parallel to my outward journey. It's deathly quiet, except for a few dogs barking in the distance. I creep three or four steps at a time and then listen. Suddenly, I see a silhouette in front of me and hear a strange sound. As I approach, it turns out to be a parachute in a small tree, inflated by the wind. Then I find a

While waiting for transport to the SAS rendezvous point at Coevorden, the French troopers stayed in the Rolde village school. Six members of stick Gramond posed for a group picture in the school yard (L-R): Soldat Stanislas Fras, Caporal-Chef Georges Lalisse (the radio operator), Sergeant Marcel Tricard, Sergeant Roger Fuzeau (who had broken his jaw in the parachute drop), Soldat Jean Molle and Soldat Marcel Legendre. (ECPAD)

The school (which stood behind the photographer) has since been replaced with a modern apartment building but the house with the thatched roof in the background still stands at No. 1 Schoolstraat. (Karel Margry)

container; so I'm now in the correct jump line. Indeed, a moment later I hear movement and I call out the French password. No answer.

"'Qui est la?'" "Le Commandant Harcourt." We're glad to have found each other. He hasn't seen anyone else yet. He has, however, located some of the containers. I tell him about my misfortune, that I'm unable to move far, that I'm only an obstacle to our mission, and that I'll take care of myself. I show him my temporary hiding place, and he says he's going to do a reconnaissance and come back to me. It's still deathly quiet. In the distance, a dog barks, and every now and then a motor vehicle passes by. A single shot, the first sign of action, then.

'I gather some camouflage material, some pine trees and heather, and around dawn, Major Harcourt returns with a parachute. It's a yellow one, however, which will only impede my cover, so I decide to suffer the cold instead. I ask him to hide it as far away as possible. Together, we choose the most suitable place for me to hide. Then he gives me his chocolate and a small bottle of rum and leaves.'

Next morning Bestebreurtje heard and saw German troops, and he had some scary moments as they searched the area around him, finding and hauling away the containers that had landed near him. He stayed in his hiding hole, feeding on pieces of chocolate en quenching his thirst from mud puddles. On the third night, he decided to move southwards, hoping to find water. Crawling for hours under great pain, he found a few sugar beets but nowhere any water and finally hid up under a stack of straw bales in an open field. Three days into his ordeal, he was discovered by a young boy, the son of farmer Jan Schutten. Next morning, father and son arrived with a horse-drawn cart and hauled Bestebreurtje to their farmhouse located on the road between Westerbork and Hooghalen. There he remained hidden in the attic until liberated by Canadian troops later that day.

His colleague, Captain Ruys van Dugteren, kept a diary of his days with the Dutch resistance group:

'Saturday, April 7, 1945

'Stick of 15 men landed at 2300 hours on a field near Hooghalen, with our team of four being the last to jump. The dispatcher was very poor, didn't know his job, and the result was a slow drop. Immediately after leaving the plane, I discovered sparks on the release box and later, upon reaching the ground, noticed that my right leg strap was loose. Because of this, when I unfastened my leg-bag, it fell straight down. I landed in a fairly wooded area and immediately started a search to locate the others and my luggage, but had no luck.

'I searched until 0400 that Sunday, after which I decided to leave the field to try and make contact. At 0600, at the drop zone, I found Teun Leever, a gamekeeper and head of the local resistance, who supported us from start to finish. After I discovered he was a suitable man, I sent him away, after he hid me in the woods, to try to locate as many people and baggage as possible. At 1000, he returned with the news that the Germans had surrounded the woods around the drop zone. Despite this, he had managed to recover several containers and also found Somers, whom he had hidden in the undergrowth

Of the four-man 'Jedburgh' team that jumped with the 2ème RCP, only two members – Dutch Captain Carel Ruys van Dugteren and British radio operator Sergeant Claude Somers – were able to contribute to the action. Picked up by forester Teun Leever, the leader of the armed resistance group of the villages of Amen and Rolde, the two men set up a command post in the woods, passing back intelligence brought in by the underground workers and organising an arms drop to the resistance. Among other things, the Dutch Interior Forces group appropriated the saloon car of SS-Brigadeführer Eberhardt Schöngarth, the Befehlshaber der Sicherheitspolizei und Sicherheitsdienst (Commander of Security Police and Security Service) in the Netherlands, which had been ambushed by stick No. 8 of the 3ème RCP under Lieutenant Edgar Tupet-Thomé along the Drentse Hoofdvaart canal on April 9. Schöngarth was the highest Gestapo officer in occupied Holland and the one responsible for the massive retaliation shootings at De Woeste Hoeve after the ambush of SS-Obergruppenführer Hanns Rauter the previous month. Soon after, the resistance group posed for the photographer with their prize (L-R): Teun Leever, 'Jedburgh' Sergeant Somers, Daan Meenken, Swijtze Postma (with hat), Hillegienus Komduur, two unidentified men, and Jan Feijen.

The picture was taken near Leever's house, vaguely seen in the background of the wartime photo. It still stands at the entrance to the Dianaheide holiday park, two kilometres south-west of Amen. Leever started this campsite after the war. (Karel Margry)

about three kilometres from where I was. Shortly afterwards, about 40 Ordnungspolizei searched the woods, but nothing was discovered, though it was close. The entire area, including the houses, was searched. When this was over, Leever went looking for Major Harcourt, who had been seen by civilians wearing American overalls. Leever had no success and went out to tell the various local resistance leaders that I wanted to speak with them that evening. He returned at 1700 with the news that 80 Jerries were approaching the woods with dogs. Leever carefully hid me and walked in a circle around where I was sitting, carrying a still-warm dead turkey. As a result, when the dogs approached the circle, they showed no interest and moved on. This action by Leever saved my life. After this, no further searches were made.

'Monday, April 9, 1945
'Leever, very active, walked back and forth day and night gathering information and approaching illegal workers. In the morning, the police commissioner of Assen reported to me on the situation in the town. The information showed that the resistance there was very poorly organised and weak. There appeared to be no KP or RVV [Knokploegen and Raad van Verzet, two Dutch resistance organisations] present, and the number of NSB members was very high. People were desperate for weapons. At 1200 hours, we sent the first messages to London, requesting arms drops as soon as possible. Leever informed us that heavy fighting was taking place between the SAS and the Germans in the Staatsbossen forest, north-east of us, and that 13 SAS men had fallen into German hands. The police here cooperated fully and proved reliable. In the distance, we heard Germans blowing up bridges over the Oranjekanaal.

'By 2000 hours, we had good contact with London; they had little hope of a successful arms drop. A girl courier from Assen said the OD [Ordedienst, another resistance organisation] leader was a wet blanket and would send his second-in-command, who wasn't very good either, but did his best. Leever, still busy, was worth his weight in gold. He searched for a suitable drop zone with a team of 20 men. A few Jerries got close, but the SAS present made things very difficult for them. We were making plans for the bridges and a telephone connection with Assen. Leever brought in very valuable information, which I passed on to London.

'Tuesday, April 10, 1945
'Delegates from Assen and the surrounding area arrived to receive the announced arms drop. A few Germans were in the area during nightly movements, but the SAS knew what to do with them. Our wireless works exceptionally well, but we're severely hampered during the day and it's quite cold.

'At 2200, all the people needed to receive the airdrop gathered in a

At the village of Zuidlaren, about midway between Assen and Groningen, stands an unusual SAS memorial. It marks the field where a stick of the 2ème RCP that had landed in the extreme north of the regimental area – No. 18 under Lieutenant Jean Lasserre – became embroiled in a fire encounter with a large German force on the morning of April 9. They had spent the night in a barn at the farm of Hindrik Hovenkamp on Lageweg but were betrayed by Harm Prins, Hovenkamp's son-in-law. One man, Soldat Paul Duquesne, was killed at the farm and ten others taken prisoner. Only Lieutenant Lasserre and four other men, one of them wounded, got away. Unveiled on April 9, 2017, on the 72nd anniversary of the action, the memorial also commemorates stick No. 19 which also came down south of Zuidlaren. Commanded by Adjutant Louis Bourrel, it found shelter at a farm along the Gieten road but the farmer, a member of the Dutch Nazi party, also betrayed their presence to the Germans and the entire stick was taken prisoner. The memorial, which names the members of both sticks, stands on Lageweg, across the road from No. 19. (Karel Margry)

nearby wood. We took off at 2230, and by 2245 everyone was in place. At 2300, right on time, our aircraft flew over, and with only one lantern as a guide, it dropped the entire load after circling twice. A tremendous feat, and all the resistance fighters were deeply impressed. We worked our tails off until 0500, and everything was hidden or distributed. A horse and cart transported the arms to Assen, where they were hidden under straw. Immediately upon our return, we provided weapons instruction, specifically for the people from Assen, who then moved off to occupy and secure the telephone line and two bridges. I wanted to go there myself, but was strongly advised against it, as there was no way I could get through. I found 17 containers with bottoms fallen out and the weapons broken or bent. Leever and two of his men stayed until daylight to cover up all traces of the drop.

'Wednesday, April 11, 1945
'More weapons training and some resistance activities against isolated Germans. Good work, very satisfied. The Jerries are getting

very nervous. Later that night, we covered a road with Bren guns and caused quite a bit of damage. Leever, more than useful, is familiar with the area. He is irreplaceable. Report on Assen satisfactory.

'Thursday, April 12, 1945
'Leever and five men harassed the Jerries all day long. The same procedure in Assen and the surrounding area, using the weapons from the airdrop. In the afternoon, tanks were sighted, heavy fighting, burning farms to the south and south-west. Rumours that Harcourt has been captured. Description of him is rather imprecise.

'Information received indicating the best route to Assen. Not via the main road from Hooghalen to Assen, but north-east, via Ekehaar and Rolde, to approach Assen from the north-east. I went south to relay this information to the Canadian vanguard, which they later used to their great satisfaction. Late in the afternoon, the Canadian tanks rolled past our farm, and everyone was overjoyed.'

On the night of April 8/9 (D+1), the one stick that had failed to take off the previous night – No. 23 of the 2ème RCP under Aspirant Pierre Lagèze – was dropped east of Smilde (i.e. some ten kilometres too far to the west and in the wrong regimental zone). One man, Sergeant Jean Marie Ravenel, got his parachute entangled with that of a container and he fell to his death. Another man, Caporal-Chef Raymond Guyon, broke his knee. The others found help, Dutch farmer Enge Voortman picking up Guyon with his horse and cart and hiding him at his farm until liberation. Enge's brother, Jan Voortman, found the rest of the stick in a wooden summerhouse, and suggested that they seize the bridge over the Drentse Hoofdvaart (known as the Veenhoopsbrug) at Smilde, which carried the Assen to Meppel main road. After some persuasion, Lagèze agreed. On the evening of April 10, the French paras silently approached the bridge, killing one German and capturing three of the bridge guard detail. Supervised by the French, Jan Voortman and another Dutchman, Jan Daling, removed the explosive charge, dropping it into the water. Thereupon the paras and their POWs withdrew back into the woods.

That evening, a strong force of 40-60 Germans returned and re-mined the bridge with explosives. The following day, April 11, they decided to blow up the span. However, the charge failed to go off, so they sent some men to fetch a new detonator from Assen. While they were away, Jan Voortman and his father boldly sneaked back to the bridge and let the explosives drop into the canal a second time. When the Germans returned, they were much surprised, and angered at the sabotage, but had no choice but to go back to Assen for yet another demolition charge. Lagèze decided to intervene. When the Germans returned in the afternoon, his stick lay waiting and opened up on them, driving them away in panic. The Germans returned in the evening but this time the paras withdrew. However, when the Germans tried to carry the explosives to the bridge in a wheelbarrow, the French

An important canal bridge that was saved by the SAS parachutists was the so-called Veenhoopsbrug over the Drentse Hoofdvaart at Smilde, six kilometres east of Appelscha. Although in the 3ème RCP zone, it was secured by a stick from its sister regiment. Aspirant Pierre Lagèze's stick No. 23 of the 2ème RCP had been unable to take off on D-Day so they jumped the following night, April 8/9. One member of the stick, Sergeant Jean Marie Ravenel, got his chute entangled with a supply container dropped by his aircraft and he fell to his death. He still lies buried in the Kerkenveld Cemetery at Smilde. (Karel Margry)

The bridge they saved was also rescued because a local man, Jan Voortman, on two occasions cut loose the demolition charge and let it drop in the water – the second time almost under the nose of the Germans! Lagèze's stick harassed the German bridge detail and, through various attacks, prevented them from re-mining and blowing the span until the arrival of the Canadian ground force.

The swing-bridge, which crossed the canal at a skew angle, has since been removed to be replaced by a modern drawbridge 100 metres south of the old one. This is where the old bridge was located.
(Karel Margry)

attacked them again. A member of Lagèze's stick, Soldat Jacques Buchart, recalled the fight:

'On April 11, at almost the same time as the day before, we carry out our third operation. This time, there are no sentries, and we take up positions near our bridge to prevent the Germans from returning and to hold the span until the end of our mission. The relative calm doesn't last very long. Two columns of Germans approach on foot, on either

The stick that landed furthest south in the 2ème RCP area was No. 4 commanded by Lieutenant Jean Sriber. They came down close to the town of Dedemsvaart, a full 45 kilometres from their prescribed drop zone. One man, Soldat Pierre Rufenacht, sprained his ankle in the jump. Learning from local Dutch where they were, they soon linked up with the Canadian ground army, scout cars of the 18th Armoured Car Regiment (12th Manitoba Dragoons) already reaching the town that same evening. For the next few days, the SAS men carried out patrols, searched the area for stray Germans and on April 11, in two separate ambushes on the Ommen to Hardenberg road, destroyed two enemy supply vehicles. In all, they captured seven German soldiers and killed or wounded four others. Prior to leaving for the rendezvous point at Coevorden, they posed for a group shot with members of the local resistance.
(Historische Vereniging Avereest 10728)

The picture was taken in front of No. 360 Langewijk, which remains completely unchanged.
(Karel Margry)

side of the canal. On Lagèze's orders we let these late-hour walkers get very close. We greet them with our automatic weapons. Our position was truly very strong. Around the bridge sentry post, the enemy had dug trenches and manholes that were extremely useful for all our actions. The main thing was always to get to them.

'So, after this cold reception, the enemy withdrew and regrouped on the other side of the canal. Next, they moved forward behind a row of houses along the canal and took up positions right across from us. Night had fallen, and tracer bullets left their fiery trails everywhere in an irregular pattern. Each side fired as the other reloaded his weapon. Then, from the trench Soldat Roger Hourdin and I were in, my ear pressed to the ground, I suddenly heard the dull sound of an engine, coming from my right. So I had to act quickly. Hourdin would cover me and fire over me, assisted by one of the newly-joined men. I lay down on the road, facing the armoured car that was slowly but surely approaching. With all my might I clamped my machine gun and fired at the target, which grew larger as it approached.

'And then the armoured car, finally hit, stopped. Part of my group had already broken off the fight. I returned to my position in the trench and fired a few rounds at targets here and there. Lagèze, rallying his men, realised that I had been left behind alone and decided to send for me. My old comrade-in-arms Hourdin did just that, crawling as close as he could towards me and shouting at me to come back.

'This action allowed the group to manoeuvre and withdraw without losses. Incidentally, the Germans also withdrew, except that they took many dead and wounded with them.'

The bridge was never blown and was still standing when the Canadian spearheads reached Smilde on the 13th.

THE 3ème RCP

THE 1er SQUADRON OF the 3ème RCP, comprising sticks Nos. 1-7, landed in the far northern corner of the regimental zone, between Assen and Norg, and found itself in a very awkward position from the start. This part of the country was very flat, cut by numerous canals and ditches, and without woods to find concealment, the only hiding places being provided by small copses and farms that dotted the countryside.

Stick No. 1, led by Lieutenant Albert Rouan, was able to assemble only 13 men, one of whom had broken a leg in the jump. Two men could not be found. With no cover anywhere, they approached a nearby farm, the Anniehoeve on Binnenweg outside the small village of Zeijerveld, and the inhabitants allowed them to hide up in a large barn, where they settled in among the straw. At dawn four Germans arrived at the farm to collect milk. They must have seen or heard something, or the farmer had betrayed the French, for two hours later a strong German force arrived, which surrounded the farm and opened up on the barn with machine guns. The Germans called on the French to surrender, and when that remained unanswered, they set fire to the barn. Hopelessly trapped, the SAS men boldly attempted a break-out but this was smothered in fire. All were taken prisoner, ten of them wounded in the hail of bullets and hand-grenades. One of the survivors, Sergeant Georges Caïtucoli, recalled the battle:

> 'The reception at the farm was very friendly. We were offered cigarettes and chocolate, and we were told we could shelter in the barn next to the farm. So we quickly summoned the rest of the group and took up positions in this building. It was chock-full of straw. From the ground floor, we couldn't see outside; there wasn't a single window. On the first floor, accessible by stairs, we could see out through windows on three sides. We had just had a rough night, after a day of preparations. So we decided to give the group some rest, but to post a guard at each window.
>
> 'Our packs, containing most of our explosives and provisions, were hidden downstairs, under the straw, and we took all our weapons and ammunition upstairs. It was probably around four in the morning. Around six o'clock, we saw four Germans arriving. They had a cart for transporting milk cans. A Dutchman came to warn us not to move, as they were only there to collect their daily supplies. We hadn't been informed of this during the conversation before we took up positions in the barn. It seemed plausible, however. Nonetheless we increased our vigilance.

The 1er Squadron of the 3ème RCP was the hardest hit of all units deployed in 'Amherst', losing 35 men killed, captured or wounded out of 105. Stick No. 1 under Lieutenant Albert Rouan thought they had found safe shelter at the Anniehoeve, a lone farm in the flat open countryside of Zeijerveld. (Karel Margry)

However, they were betrayed and a German force with machine guns surrounded the barn where they had hid up (seen here at centre). They refused all calls for surrender and, when the Germans set fire to the barn, made a desperate attempt to break out. Caught in a hail of bullets and hand-grenades, ten of them were wounded and the entire stick was taken prisoner. (Karel Margry)

A small metal plaque, affixed to the barn wall by the French SAS Veterans Association, commemorates the tragedy. (Karel Margry)

'Around eight o'clock, we were awakened by a loud commotion, without realising that enemy groups had approached us. There were numerous blind spots in the barn, with entire sections hidden from view. The Germans, well aware of this, had taken advantage of this by taking up positions on three sides.

'They began firing heavily at us with five machine guns; fire that caused no harm but, to put it mildly, surprised us unpleasantly.

'We weathered out the storm. The situation was very clear. We assessed the situation, Rouan and I. Given the early hour, it seemed impossible that we could hold out until evening. We were trapped, and the terrain gave us little hope.

'Indeed, the Germans were in one of the outbuildings and to the left and right of our barn, hidden behind a shed with farm wagons and behind a tall building. They surrounded us on three sides and had left the area in front of the barn, which was completely open, unoccupied. Entering that area was tantamount to committing suicide.

'About ten minutes had passed after the first shots, and we wondered what would happen next. There was more shooting, just as heavy as the first. Then, after a ten-minute interlude, again.

'In the barn, we had taken up positions by the windows and were covering the door with our automatic weapons in case they tried to force their way in there, which was highly unlikely by the way. After another ten-minute wait, the Germans, speaking over a loudspeaker in broken but understandable French, called out to us: "Frenchmen, we know you are in there, surrender, we will spare your lives."

'We decided not to answer at all. Besides, we hadn't fired a single shot yet, as we wanted to save our ammunition and, moreover, we hadn't seen a single German yet.

'Lieutenant Rouan and I isolated ourselves for a moment, because we had to make a decision no matter what. Our mission was over. There was no way the 13 SAS men, cooped up in a barn, in an area without cover, could first escape and then carry out the main mission or some other subsidiary mission, with the Wehrmacht hot on their heels. And all that 150 to 200 kilometres behind the Allied lines.

'Rouan straightaway said to me: "We are not surrendering." I said: "Okay, we're going to inform everyone." We all gathered around. We explained what we wanted to do, and everyone gave their opinion. It was simple: everyone agreed there was no other solution.

'Now that this was settled, we had to try to hold out. We knew the Germans wouldn't enter the barn. On the other hand, they were out of our reach. We had made a hole in the roof to reduce our blind spots, and this allowed us to see some of the German movements and discover most of their positions.

'So we let half an hour pass and even began to think that, given the way things were going and if it got dark soon, we might still have a small chance. After that half hour, they repeated their call, adding that it was the last one. We destroyed all our radio equipment and our secret codes. We took the most important things from our packs, that is, only ammunition and grenades. If we were to get away, we could only do so with light equipment. After that, we waited.

'Around half past nine, we realised we had to act quickly. Very dense smoke poured into the barn, which they had set on fire in three different places. We had expected it.

'In front of the barn was a small shed, on the left was a wagon shed where the Germans were, and on the right was a manure-pit with a pigsty nearby. We had decided to get out in two waves: first, my group, which would occupy part of the area by taking up positions to the left and right of the exit, and then Rouan's group.

'When we gave the order, we immediately raised both handles on the barn door, threw grenades left and right with the safety pins already removed, and, firing in all directions, rushed outside. That's how I managed to reach the right-hand corner of the barn, directly opposite the pigsty. With my American carbine, I tried to neutralise the Germans who were in the centre part of the farmhouse on the other side. But they had snipers stationed at the windows. We had located them from the barn by one of the openings we had broken through the roofing. Those snipers were my first target, and they didn't stay there.

'When I turned to see what was happening behind me, I noticed Rouan lying on his back on a pile of straw opposite the barn door. I ran towards him. He had a bullet in his chest, and the pile of straw was on fire. I dragged him to the barn door and then, helped by Sergeant Bolusset, to the pigsty, which had a hard-surface floor.

'From the pigsty, I tried to shoot a German who was at the end of the wagon shed. The only accessible point of cover was the manure-pit. I yelled at everyone to get there, but unfortunately, only a few could reach it.

'From the manure-pit, I could see – or rather Bolusset pointed this out to me – that 15 metres ahead of us, a German was sitting in a manhole, repeatedly firing at us with a sub-machine gun. These holes were single-man shelters that the Dutch had dug almost everywhere around their farm. First, as shelter from bombardments and secondly as places to find cover in during ground combat.

'After Bolusset pointed out the spot to me, I decided to throw a grenade. I was known to be quite good at it. My grenade landed ten centimetres from the hole and had no effect whatsoever. Of course, it would have been different if it had fallen in. It was my last one; I'd thrown the other one as I came out the barn door. For five or 20 minutes, shots were fired intermittently, and in the end only three men remained unharmed in the manure-pit. We were out of ammunition. So the firing stopped and the Germans came to take us prisoner.

'Lieutenant Rouan had been hit by a bullet that had passed through his chest from above, just behind the heart. Sergeant François Command had a bullet in his shoulder. Caporal André Bergamaschi had a bullet in his right hand, one in his right arm and one in his right thigh. Sergeant Henri Mouton had a broken leg and a bullet in his thigh. Soldat André Favir had a bullet in his right leg, Sergeant René Bolusset had one in his ankle, and Caporal Jacques Coulon one in his throat. Caporal Jean Savelli had shrapnel in his face, legs and back, and Soldat Maurice Chataux in his hand. Caporal Paul Fouet thought he was going to die because a bullet had hit him right in the chest, but it had been stopped by his wallet and his dog-tag. Caporal Pierre Schmidt, Soldat Marc Bajolet-Pilgrain and I were practically unharmed, except that I had a cut on my right wrist.

'How and why can one endure such shooting? That's what one sometimes wonders. The Germans asked us to care for our wounded, and I was mainly concerned with Rouan, who was in very bad shape. The bullet had exited his body straight through the back, creating a huge hole that I managed to plug with bandages from our backpacks, which the Germans had retrieved from the barn. In the end only half of the barn was burned down. The wounded were put together in a corner of the meadow and we were gathered nearby.'

Stick No. 2, led by Lieutenant Joseph Ferchaud, landed on top of a German convoy moving along the Assen to Groningen main road and was completely scattered, most of the men being taken prisoner and only Ferchaud making good his escape.

Stick No. 3 under Sous-Lieutenant Jean Valayer landed inside Assen, coming down among houses of Sluisstraat on the western edge of town. Finding ten Germans in a nearby farm shed, they quickly took them prisoner. One man in the stick had broken an ankle, and Sergeant Marc Loï was missing (he would survive in hiding in Assen until liberation). Guided by farmer Lammert Slofstra, Valayer and his 12 troopers started out westwards towards their assigned DZ, taking their prisoners along. After tramping through the night, they hid up in an isolated barn on Koelenweg belonging to the Mulder farm. By then, Valayer had lost the tail of his stick (including two of the POWs) and had only two of his men left, Sergeant Jean-Jacques Doal and Soldat Ibrahim Azem. However, during the morning four strays from other sticks joined them: Soldats Marcel Lévêque and Robert Spina (from Rouan's stick No. 1), Soldat Jean Pierre Munch (stick No. 5) and Caporal Pierre Bévalot (stick No. 7). Later that morning farmer Reint Mulder discovered the men, and soon a small crowd of civilians stood outside the barn, fraternising with the paras.

Valayer and his men stayed in the barn throughout Sunday and Monday. However, the man assigned to guard the eight POWs on the first night fell asleep and, on waking up, found that they had escaped. It was either them or two Dutch Landwachters who had passed with a horse and cart on Sunday that went to alert the Germans, for early on Tuesday (April 10) a force of Germans and Landwachters surrounded the barn and opened up with machine guns. After an hour, they fired tracer bullets into the thatched roof which set the building on fire. Hopelessly trapped, the seven paras attempted a break-out on both sides of the barn. However, the doors at one end were locked and the men here, Valayer, Munch and Spina, burned to death inside the building. Azem, Bévalot and Lévêque were killed as they

An almost identical but even more deadly tragedy occurred at another barn, less than two kilometres away from the Anniehoeve. Farmer Reint Mulder had a stand-alone barn on Koelenweg. Here on April 10, seven men under Lieutenant Jean Valayer, the leader of stick No. 3, were also betrayed, the barn was also surrounded by a force of Germans and Dutch collaborators and then set on fire, but when the men inside tried to break out, the door at one end turned out to be blocked and three men burned to death inside the burning building. Of the four that managed to get out on the other side, three were killed and one captured. The incinerated remains of the three men who perished inside the barn – Valayer, Soldat Jean Pierre Munch and Soldat Robert Spina – were buried near the fire-ruined building.

The barn was rebuilt and a house added on to it later. (Karel Margry)

Today, a cross and a plaque on the barn commemorate the names of the six victims. (Karel Margry)

rushed out on their side. Only Doal survived, out of ammunition and being taken prisoner. (The other ten men of Valayer's stick, under Sous-Lieutenant Robert Raillard, would hold out near Bovensmilde until link-up with the ground force on the 13th).

Stick No. 4, led by Sous-Lieutenant Pierre Poli-Marchetti, was dropped the furthest north of all, coming down between the villages of Norg and Peest. As they searched for their containers, they came across a small airfield (the Lufwaffe reserve airfield of Peest), which they saw was heavily guarded. A mid-morning, one half-stick went to look for their objective, reputed to be a V1 launching site. They found an installation which they thought was their target and, although it looked dismantled, made sure to destroy it. (Allied intelligence was wrong. In actual fact, there were no V1 sites in this part of Holland). At dusk, the stick encountered German troops searching the area and in the ensuing firefight four men, including Lieutenant Poli-Marchetti, were separated from the group. Sergeant Charles Lévêque took charge of the stick and the following morning, with the help of two young Dutchmen, Albertus Bosscha and Ide Hoff, found a good place to hide up. Sergeant Lévêque recalls meeting the two Dutchmen:

> 'Early in the morning, I awoke to the sound of voices. I couldn't clearly distinguish between Dutch and German, both of which are languages with quite a few guttural sounds, and I was ready to give them a good reception. Then I met two Dutchmen, Hoff and Bosscha.
>
> 'At that same moment, I became aware that my stick was in a precarious situation. The dense forest with, as I had thought the day before, abundant vegetation was nothing more than a birch grove with young spring foliage and ridiculously thin trunks.
>
> 'The two men seemed shy and, like me, spoke only broken English. They first led us to a less-conspicuous and safer spot. No sign of Sous-Lieutenant Poli-Marchetti and the others. Poli-Marchetti had joined the 3ème RCP and the 1er Squadron during our operations in France. He came from the Résistance in the Rhône region and, unlike most of us, had not received SAS training. I was worried about him. So I took command of the stick. My first concern was to find a safe place, because our skirmish the day before must have unnerved the Germans; the men also had to eat and we were to gather intelligence on enemy activity and movements. Suspicious by nature, I cautiously accepted the cooperation of these two young men. Until they returned we remained on our guard, especially since artillery fire and gunshots could be heard coming from the spot we had come from, apparently at very close range, which didn't bode well.
>
> 'When we awoke, the Germans simply destroyed the copse, our first bivouac area. It wasn't the time to linger there so we moved to another camp. This was how it went throughout the seven difficult days we endured in the Netherlands.

'On the second day Bosscha finally found us again. He proved to be a valuable chap. He brought provisions and bread, which, although black, was very tasty. He warned us that we were being hunted and that we had to be careful in everything we did. I also asked him for civilian clothes, because I didn't want to be constantly at risk of being attacked. So, that evening, accompanied by Hoff and Bosscha, I set out, leaving the camp area to the chaplain [Aspirant François Gagey, the regimental padre who had jumped with the stick], who guarded it closely. I wore overalls over my military uniform, had clogs on my feet and a cap on my head. My only weapon was my Colt, which I wore hidden on my chest. I carried a dagger on my leg. I saw the encampment again, razed to the ground, but there hadn't been any digging in it. So, in principle, the ammunition we had buried there was still there, a conclusion I didn't share with my companions. Then, in Norg, I made a map study of the area, and we went across country to visit the family of Hoff or of Bosscha, I don't remember. There were 300 Germans in Norg, 500 in Peest, and there were few locals on our side. Here and there we heard gunfire; clearly other sticks were active.

'Upon our return to the camp there was no news. Each stick was equipped with a radio receiver, and we had to listen in four times a day at fixed times. 'Roméo' [SAS headquarters in England] would send messages or give orders to the 'Jeanettes' [code-name for the sticks]. Our call-sign was 'Jeanette 108,' but Roméo hadn't been heard from yet. The small radio had been entrusted to Caporal Gilbert Grécias, a quiet boy. He was a young high school student from Algiers, officially 21 years old but actually only 18. The device measured 20 by 10 centimetres and was worn in a case fastened to the chest. It had headphones under a hood that served as an antenna.

'Because we were completely independent, we had to carry out a main mission and in addition create confusion wherever possible. Although the main missions weren't always successfully executed, creating chaos worked better than we could have hoped. During the day, we were chased by patrols, but at night we set ambushes. We did so for a convoy of horse-drawn carts transporting fuel, escorted by German troops who were singing to conceal their fear. We also carried out acts of sabotage at the airfield. Departing for a 48-hour mission, we had, all told, two boxes of the famous 24-hour rations with us, one box per day. And Benzedrine tablets to pep up an exhausted man. The rations quickly ran out. Moreover, the men couldn't muster the patience to dissolve the pills in the water they drank, and so six men soon contracted dysentery, reducing them to little more than human wrecks.

'And still nothing, not a single message. Hoff and Bosscha did what they could. We ate raw potatoes, which we stole from silos, and we sucked on the stems of the tubers that were so common in this area.'

For the next week, the SAS men lay low during the day and laid road ambushes at night. On the fourth day, the four missing men re-joined them, hungry and exhausted from being chased. Not until April 14, the seventh day, were they finally overrun by Canadian forces.

Stick No. 5 under Capitaine Charles Picard, the squadron commander, on landing found that they were in a wide expanse of fields completely devoid of cover. Four men were missing (Lieutenant De Sablet, drowned; Soldat Munch, killed with Valayer; Soldat Jean-Marie Battesti, captured by the Germans, and Soldat Marcel Fabert, killed in a lone encounter with the Germans at nearby Zuidvelde). Finding that he was five kilometres south of his DZ, Picard led his men north and at daybreak hid up in an area of low underbrush known as De Fledders near the Norgervaart canal. There they stayed for another six days, passing back information via their wireless set and attempting to lay ambushes on the roads at night, until finally relieved by Canadian forces on April 13. Picard left a good account of his group's arrival and stay at De Fledders:

> 'Although it's starting to get light, I guide my stick west, toward a small copse I found on the map, two or three kilometres away. Despite our

Capitaine Charles Picard, the 1er Squadron commander, found on assembly that his stick leader was missing (Lieutenant De Sablet, drowned in an irrigation ditch near Smilde – see page 32) and that he was well off his target. With the flat open countryside offering little or no cover, they eventually hid up in an area of low underbrush known as De Fledders and for the next six days attempted to mount ambushes and radio back intelligence on enemy columns passing their hide-out. These snapshots were taken on the first day. Front left in this one is Caporal Jean-Pierre Salvatori.

Picard (centre) and his men with Jacob Lubbers (with cap), a Dutch farmer who together with his son Jan was held in custody for a while by the French.

heavy packs, we're traveling at a brisk pace, through completely open terrain, but apparently unnoticed at this early hour. Following a dirt road, we reach a spot flanked by some vegetation resembling low brush.

'Since I don't want to risk advancing in broad daylight, I decide not to go any further. A few of the men are deployed at the edge of the copse to monitor the terrain and allow the rest of the stick to rest. As the day progresses, we repeatedly hear shots and bursts from automatic weapons. We also see German patrols coming and going on a nearby road. In our precarious and vulnerable shelter, which perhaps thanks to its mediocre quality went unnoticed during the enemy's hunt for the parachutists, the men stand on the look-out, ready to fight, but nothing happens.

'Nothing happens, except that late in the morning, along the road we are occupying, a Dutch civilian of about 30 years old arrives. He is visibly surprised to find us there. He says he's out for a walk, which isn't strange, for after all it's a Sunday. But I'm suspicious. He argues that he's trustworthy and would like to leave, because otherwise they'll be worried at home. That's out of the question, because even if he's not pro-German, he'll undoubtedly talk. So he'll stay with us for a large part of this long day, which he ultimately accepts with the necessary resignation.

'Things get serious when, around mid-afternoon, two girls, aged 18 to 20, also out for a walk, arrive, astonished to see us. They seem very nice, but caution is advised. Because I suspect they won't be able to keep their mouths shut, I decide to detain them as well. They take it well and liven up our situation a bit.

'Just before dusk, I release the three forced guests, assuming that if they talk and their words reach the Germans, it will be too late to launch an action against us. They undoubtedly did not hesitate to tell of their adventure and I am sure captivated their audience, but it didn't harm us.

'Evening is coming. Night is falling at last. A long-awaited night, one that brings safety and freedom of movement. I send my first radio message to our headquarters in England, to pass on the information we gathered during the night in the house where we received such a warm welcome and what we gathered during the day thanks to our unexpected visitors.

> 'Then, I go out with my stick to thoroughly comb the area, my plan being to fire on convoys on the roads. But that night nothing moves, and on the deserted roads we search in vain for an opportunity, waiting fruitlessly for a chance to engage in battle. This is of course very disappointing. But it's less unsatisfactory when you consider that for an enemy forced to retreat by the unstoppable Allied advance, this lack of mobility is caused by the uncertainty created by Operation 'Amherst', with its airdrops conducted over a wide area and the resulting misleading impression regarding the strength of the troops actually deployed.
>
> 'Before dawn, the stick returns to the hiding place, which the past day has given us confidence in. We make it a bit more spacious by adding a small plot of undeveloped heathland, where we can hide, provided we stay in a crawling position. During the day, I contact a neighbouring farmer. He's clearly a patriot. He briefs me specifically on the events of the day before. Throughout the day the Germans searched for parachutists. It appears they have found some of them in the woods along the Norgervaart canal. A little later, he brings us a pan of potatoes, a tasty addition to the bland food from the British Army rations.
>
> 'Ultimately, the stick will remain in that shelter, which offers rather cramped space and such limited security that it cannot be considered a proper base of operations. But apparently there's nothing better, at least not in the area assigned to the squadron. Besides, in our neighbour, the farmer, we have a very useful informant, who also provides us with supplies. And from that point on, the stick will operate on the roads where the Germans have resumed their movements, firing on and delaying passing convoys, forcing them to stop and fight to shake off the enemy.'

Stick No. 6, led by Sous-Lieutenant Paul-Marie Boiteux, came down 18 kilometres south of its planned DZ, and south of the Oranjekanaal. With daylight, they spotted a large factory building, the potato-flour mill at Oranje. A Dutch cyclist told them it housed a German unit and that there was a bridge across the canal in front of it. By now civilians had found their containers but the Bren guns in them had first to be degreased. That done, they went to scout out the mill but, as they approached, the Germans opened fire on them and five of the SAS men were captured, one of them wounded. One of Boiteux's men, Soldat Philippe Paris, recalled the failed action:

> 'We are split into two groups. Mine consists of Soldat Jean Auteuil and Caporal Norbert Benchemoul, nicknamed Briquet. With Sergeant Pierre Julliard are Soldats Georges Chaboche, Arthur Frelon, Robert

Pacaud and Fernand Bridon. We move forward, towards the left side of the factory, to provide flanking cover for the other group, which will attack the bridge. Just as the assault begins, armed men emerge from the buildings opposite us and a fierce firefight ensues. From a shed and from behind an embankment we take the far bank of the canal under fire. Because the Germans are using small boats, threatening to cut off our retreat, Benchemoul orders a withdrawal. I had ducked down in a drainage ditch. Under a hail of bullets I jump over the embankment in one bound. My comrades understand that under these circumstances it will be suicidal for them to follow my example. Because the enemy has now ranged in on us, they advise me to take off and try my luck alone. They will be captured shortly.

'For a long time and at a slow pace I crawled in the direction of my other comrades. Slowly the sounds of battle died down. I got to my feet and ran to a copse before trying to re-join the rest of my stick.

'Barely had I reached it when I was surrounded and captured by about ten SS men. They took me aboard a ship moored a few hundred metres away, where the canal ran through a wood. There they robbed me of all my personal belongings. To my surprise, I saw Frelon again, who was wounded, and Chaboche, who told me that they had carried out their orders, neutralised the guards, and thrown the torpedoes [attached to the bridge as explosives] into the water. But like us, they had been unable to withdraw and had lost contact with the rest of the stick because they had been attacked in the flank by Germans who had crossed in a small boat.'

Pulling back, the other members of the stick found refuge in a farm barn. Sergeant Pierre Juillard detracted the pursuing Germans by opening fire from the outside, being wounded and captured in the act, but stopping the Germans from searching any further. After they had left, the remaining nine SAS men made the barn their base from where they laid night ambushes for four days until overrun by the Canadians on the 12th.

Stick No. 7, commanded by Lieutenant François Boulon, came down near the correct DZ but landed almost on top of a German convoy moving on the Assen to Norg road and, on assembling, found that one man was missing (Caporal Bévalot, subsequently killed with Valayer). They set up a base in a small wood near the village of Norg but on the second day, April 9, were attacked by a German force with machine guns, grenade-launchers and flame-throwers. Three men were wounded, one of them, Soldat André Boudé, dying of his wounds. The remnant of the stick moved east, towards Assen, but early next morning (April 10) was again attacked by Dutch SS. Three more men were wounded and all were captured. Two of them, Lieutenant Boulon and Soldat Robert Dedieu, were executed alongside Soldat Jean Loeillet (from stick No. 22 of the 2ème RCP), one German and ten civilians (seven resistance men and three black marketeers) in the Assen

On April 10, three captured parachutists – Lieutenant François Boulon and Soldat Robert Dedieu from stick No. 7 of the 3ème RCP and Soldat Jean Loeillet from stick No. 22 of the 2ème RCP, together with ten Dutch civilians and one German were executed in the Assen municipal sports grounds on Stadsbroek. A memorial marks the site today.

municipal sports grounds later that day. Only five men escaped capture, being overrun on the 13th.

In all, the 1er Squadron suffered the highest losses of any SAS squadron in 'Amherst': 11 killed, at least 27 captured (13 of them wounded) plus one more wounded – 39 men out of 105, a loss rate of 37 per cent.

Further south in the 3ème RCP sector, the 2ème Squadron was mainly tasked with securing bridges. One of the most-successful ones was stick No. 12 under Lieutenant Maurice Duno. Dropped not far from their DZ, they took five hours to assemble. As they marched eastwards to their objective, the village of Smilde, they passed through the village of Appelscha where they found a sturdy draw-bridge (the so-called Stokersverlaatbrug) over the Opsterlandse Compagnonsvaart canal. It was undamaged and unguarded, so Duno decided to dig in and try to hold it. With a wood just two kilometres away, he felt safe enough in case a hiding place was needed against a stronger enemy force.

For the next three days, Duno and his 14 men held on to the bridge, shooting up German vehicles that unsuspectingly approached their position. The first one, a car that emerged out of the village that first morning, was riddled by Duno's Bren gunner, killing the occupants, one of them a major. The second one, appearing the following morning and engaged at 100 metres' distance, stopped and two Germans emerged with their hands up, one of them again a major. The third, a bus that approached on the road running parallel with the canal from the direction of Smilde, was first halted with two Gammon

'Amherst' was all about securing bridges for the Canadian ground force. However, with the Germans blowing virtually every one of the 150-odd bridges in the province, the SAS were able to secure only very few. A resounding success was achieved at the village of Appelscha, where Lieutenant Maurice Duno and his men of stick No. 12 of the 3ème RCP seized and held the drawbridge over the Opsterlandse Compagnonsvaart canal.

The Stokersverlaatbrug as it is called remains exactly as it was in 1945.

Local doctor Willem Gerlach had a camera and he took numerous snapshots. Here Duno and his men stand at the northern end of the bridge. The traffic signs giving directions to Assen, Meppel and Steenwijk are indicative of the bridge's importance to regional traffic. (Willem Gerlach)

The house that stood at the northern end of the bridge – the bakery of Hendrik Stoker – has been pulled down, the gap creating space for a new road leading northwards. (Karel Margry)

bombs, one in front of the vehicle and one behind, and then engaged with the Bren. One occupant was killed, the others surrendered. Lieutenant Duno recalled the three incidents:

> 'April 8
> 'Around 9 a.m., a German vehicle appears from Appelscha directly opposite the bridge. From 50 meters away, the Bren gun opens fire. The vehicle overturns and lands in the ditch. The occupants, including a major, are killed. All day long we search with patrols within a three-kilometre radius for other parachutists but in vain. However, we do capture three isolated Germans. Given our limited strength, we remain cautious as we could face a formidable enemy at any moment.
>
> 'April 9
> 'I decide Appelscha will be the base for our operations. Around 10 a.m., a vehicle appears, just like the day before. Upon spotting the car in the ditch, the driver slows down. We open fire at 100 metres, the vehicle stops, and two Germans get out with their hands up. One

Duno's men pictured in front of the house. (Willem Gerlach)

of them, a major, has been wounded in the face. The vehicle is quickly searched. In the officer's map case is a list of Dutch-sounding names of resistance fighters imprisoned in Groningen.

'During the day, Dutch people come to us. One claims to be an officer in the Dutch Army and a member of the resistance movement. We show him the SS officer. He looks at the list the man was carrying and tells us it concerns resistance fighters who were to be executed. We hand the two Germans over to him.

'In the course of minor skirmishes we capture five or six more men. They present us with a guarding problem. Then a farmer, who lives about 300 to 400 metres away, offers us his pigsty, from which the Germans have shortly before requisitioned the last pig. They will be guarded by two SAS men. The farmer was a great help to us and showed true courage for his fate would not have been enviable if things had gone badly.

'April 10

'A German motor-bus from Smilde comes into sight in the distance. It is driving on the road on the south side

And at the garage of the Café Hulst on the other side of the canal. (Willem Gerlach)

Among the parachutists at Appelscha were two brothers, (L-R) Caporal Jean-Pierre and Soldat Jean Laborderie, both from stick No. 12 of the 3ème RCP. (Willem Gerlach)

> of the canal. Because we want to capture it undamaged, we prepare our action carefully. When the vehicle is 20 meters away two Gammon bombs explode, one in front of it and one behind. The vehicle stops. A short machine-gun salvo follows, aimed at passenger level. One man is killed, several are wounded, the others surrender and are taken to the farm, as is the bus, which has not sustained any serious damage and will be hidden there. We hope it will be useful for our movements.'

Throughout this period, the stick sent out patrols, looking for other paras and capturing isolated Germans. On the third day, they contacted Capitaine

On the third day, April 10, a patrol sent out by Duno contacted Capitaine Pierre Sicaud, the 2ème Squadron commander, who had collected men from various sticks in a wood south of Appelscha. They joined Duno's force at the bridge. Here Sicaud (centre) holds up a Dutch flag to which a small banner with the Cross of Lorraine, symbol of the Free French, has been tied. (Willem Gerlach)

The two houses on the far bank stand unchanged. (Karel Margry)

Dutch underground workers, members of the Knokploeg Drenthe-Noord (with white armbands), proudly pose with their allies and liberators (L-R): Jan Bulthuis, unknown, Ritze Vos, unknown, Soldat Albert Rambeau, Sous-Lieutenant Pierre Bourdon (from stick No. 11), Sous-Lieutenant Louis Brunet (from stick No. 13), Dinie Vos and Sergeant Bernard Maurisset. Kneeling are Soldat Francis Roma and an unidentified trooper. (Willem Gerlach)

People pass into history but bicycles remain. In 1952, both Jan Bulthuis and Ritze Vos were awarded the Dutch Bronze Cross for their resistance work. (Karel Margry)

Sicaud, their squadron commander, who was still blinded from the drop, and who had assembled men from various sticks in a Dutch resistance hide-out (known as the 'Prince Bernhard Barracks') south of Appelscha. Sicaud decided to have his force join Duno's stick at the bridge, making the Café Hulst his command post. By that day, the total number of Germans captured had reached 47. Tjamme Rooks, a farmer who lived 400 metres from the

On April 13, a troop of armoured cars of the Canadian 18th Armoured Car Regiment (12th Manitoba Dragoons) reached Appelscha and relieved the SAS force. This Staghound was pictured on the northern bank of the canal. In the background stands the Mulder Brothers flour-mill, on the roof of which the SAS men had set up a machine-gun post. (Willem Gerlach)

The flour-mill remains to link past and present. The view is westwards. (Karel Margry)

bridge, had offered his pigsty and this is where they were kept, guarded by two paras.

With so many men, and so many prisoners, Sicaud radioed for resupply and two Typhoon fighter-bombers of No. 146 Wing dropped four supply containers on April 11. Two days later, on the 13th, armoured cars of the Canadian 18th Armoured Car Regiment (12th Manitoba Dragoons) reached Appelscha and relieved the SAS force.

Locals swarm around the Canadian vehicles in front of the Stoker bakery – now unfortunately no longer standing. (Willem Gerlach)

On the south bank of the canal, a few metres from the bridge, today stands a memorial to the Régiment de Chasseurs Parachutistes SAS. It was unveiled in April 2015 on the 70th anniversary of the liberation. (Karel Margry)

Another stick of the 3ème RCP, No. 13 led by Lieutenant Albert Vidoni, came down near the village of Haulerwijk, 12 kilometres north-west of Appelscha. Having captured four Germans at a farm, they proceeded to shoot them in cold blood – an act that abhorred the Dutch locals who witnessed it. After dawn, the stick was attacked by a large German force. One man was killed, five were captured, four of them wounded, and the rest of the stick was dispersed. Soldat Henri Pintaud is today commemorated on the war memorial in the Eikenhof Cemetery in Haulerwijk. (Karel Margry)

Lieutenant Vidoni, wounded in the hand and now all on his own, found refuge in the villa of Lambertus Kok, the burgomaster of Oosterwolde. Although a member of the Dutch Nazi party, Kok did not betray him but warned the local doctor who treated Vidoni's wound and notified the local resistance. Their leader, Roel Voortman, brought Vidoni to another safe house in the village of Haule where he stayed for three days. On April 13, Voortman took Vidoni and two other stray SAS troopers that he had picked up – Caporal Raymond Hauser and one other man from Lieutenant De Sablet's stick No. 5 – on bicycles to join Capitaine Sicaud's group at Appelscha. En route there, in the village of Oosterwolde, they were photographed amid a swarm of excited civilians by the local dentist, Homme Zuidersma. On the bikes are (L-R) Caporal Hauser, the unidentified trooper (behind Hauser), Roel Voortman (carrying Vidoni's rifle) and Vidoni (with hand in sling).
(Homme Zuidersma)

The photo was taken in the centre of the town, on the corner of Brinkstraat with Molenweg, just short of the canal bridge. (Karel Margry)

Above: **Patrolling the woods south of Appelscha, men of Lieutenant Edmond Hubler's stick No. 9 of the 3ème RCP came across a Jewish family from Amsterdam who had been in hiding in a forest hut since December 1943. Jozef and Mietje Lezer and their two children, 17-year-old Mia and eight-year-old Philip, were elated to see their liberators.** *Above right:* **Here, mother and daughter pose with Lieutenant Hubler.** *Right:* **Mia and her mother with the other officer in the stick, Sous-Lieutenant Marc Boyé (far right).**
(Wybo Boersma Collection)

Acted out in the last month of the war, 'Amherst' witnessed the brutal oppression that characterised the last stage of the Nazi occupation of Holland. The Germans reacted ruthlessly to the landings, burning down farms and executing civilians suspected of having assisted the SAS troopers. One such incident occurred at the village of Diever, 16 kilometres south of Appelscha. In the afternoon of April 10, a company-size German force was preparing to enter the village to quench unrest that had arisen between locals, who considered themselves liberated by the French paras encamped in the nearby woods, and Dutch Nazi sympathisers. Just at that moment a patrol from Lieutenant Edgar Tupet-Thomé's stick No. 8 of the 3ème RCP, who had been alerted by a local resistance leader, opened up on the Germans at the eastern end of the village, killing and wounding several. Realising the size of the enemy force, the French soon broke off the fight and Thomé quickly moved his bivouac deeper into the woods. However, the Germans, enraged by the incident, descended on the village, randomly rounded up 11 male inhabitants, lined them up and shot them out of hand. One man, Koop Westerhof, miraculously survived the execution. Hit by two bullets, he played dead until he could get away after dark. Today a monument on Bosweg, on the spot where the executions took place, commemorates the ten victims. (Karel Margry)

Another stick of the 2ème Squadron, No. 8 under Lieutenant Edgar Tupet-Thomé, came down near the Berkenheuvel wood outside the village of Diever, 12 kilometres south of Appelscha. On the second day, April 9, they ambushed several German vehicles on the road along the Drentse Hoofdvaart canal, including a motorcycle combination that turned out to contain important documents. They also, in company with men from Capitaine Sicaud's stick, attacked a German barge and a river tug that came sailing up the canal, sinking both vessels with grenades and Gammon bombs and killing or capturing the crews. That same afternoon, at the request of the local resistance, they went out to arrest the collaborationist burgomaster of Diever, Pier Obe Posthumus, tying him to a tree. However, the following day, just as they were engaging a group of Germans at the eastern end of the village, a much-larger German force, about 150 strong, fell down on Diever, forcing the French to disengage. In an act of reprisal, the enraged Germans arrested 11 civilians, lined them up along the edge of the local cemetery and summarily shot them. Only one man survived the execution. Thomé's men retreated further into the woods, and subsequently joined Sicaud's and Duno's force in Appelscha.

An even worse incident occurred that same day further south in the 3ème RCP area. Stick No. 14 of the 2ème RCP under Sous-Lieutenant Francis Nicol had landed in the Spaarbankbos woods near the hamlet of Toldijk, just north of Hoogeveen (ten kilometres south-west of its assigned DZ), and assembled at the farm of Jan Vos on Wijsterseweg. Heavily attacked by German troops from the town on April 9, they broke off the fight and moved eastwards, guided by a Dutchman, Koert Dekker. After they had gone, the Germans searched all the farms on Wijsterseweg, shooting three members of the Scholing family and fatally wounding the mother. They then rounded up 15 men suspected of having helped the French and marched them off northwards. That evening, at Eursinge, one man, Hayo Wubs, tried to escape but he was shot. The following morning, April 10, the group reached the small village of Spier, where they were handed over to a detachment of Ordnungspolizei under command of a man named Jung. Shortly afterwards, the 14 men were led a short distance into the woods and executed. Today, there are two memorials commemorating the tragedy, one on Wijsterseweg at the farms where the men were rounded up *(above left and right)* and one just north of Spier where the 14 were shot *(below left and right)*. The former, dedicated in April 2011, lists the 19 victims from this community. The cross at Spier, already unveiled in April 1948, included two more men found shot in the Spaarbankbos wood and thus states the number of victims as 21. (Karel Margry)

The day after the murder of the civilians, Spier became a scene of combat when a large group from the 3ème RCP under the command of the battalion commander, Lieutenant-Colonel Jacques de Bollardière, occupied the crossroad village. They had come from the nearby woods where five sticks had congregated and where this picture was taken. Looking into the camera on the left is Major Jean Simon, the battalion second-in-command, who would be killed at Spier a few hours later. (ECPAD)

Some 12 kilometres to the south-east from Diever in the 3ème RCP sector, five sticks of the Squadron de Commandement (HQ Squadron) all came down not far from the Meppel to Assen main road, north and south of the village of Spier. The sticks involved were Nos. 19 (Lieutenant-Colonel De Bollardière, the battalion commander), 20 (Capitaine Gilbert Paumier), 21 (Sous-Lieutenant Jacques Dreyfus), 22 (Capitaine Claude Vallières) and 23 (Sous-Lieutenant Lothaire Grumbach).

Colonel De Bollardière set up a command post in the woods west of Spier and gave out orders for sticks and individual stray soldiers to assemble there. By the third day, April 10, his force had grown to about 30-40 men and, expecting the arrival of the Canadian ground force shortly, he decided to occupy Spier. Positioned astride a main road, the crossroad village was obviously an important objective. De Bollardière asked for air support but this was refused because of the policy of 'not shooting up Dutch villages unless it was a tactical necessity'. He decided to go ahead anyway.

That evening, his men attacked the village, driving out the enemy, killing some and capturing a few, at the cost of two wounded. On one corner of the Spier crossroads stood the Café Ten Buur. In the preceding week it had been a German command post and the Germans had built a large open dugout across the road from it. Here the paras took up position.

The following morning, numerous curious civilians were milling around

The French troops dug in around the crossroads, making use of a large earthwork that the Germans had constructed for use as an emplacement for an anti-tank gun. At rear is the Café Ten Buur. (Wybo Boersma Collection)

The café, today Brasserie Spier, still stands at the crossroads. (Karel Margry)

Major Simon was killed when a large German force attacked Spier from the north, having just taken over manning a Bren gun after its operator, Sergeant Claude Campan, got a bullet in the head. Today, a symbolic field grave by the side of the road marks the spot where the two men fell.

For over six decades, the plaque named only Simon but in 2010 the text was amended to incorporate Campan's name as well.
(Karel Margry)

the crossroads so when Pieter Cort van der Linden, the former mayor of Groningen (who was in hiding from the Germans), reported in, De Bollardière asked him to organise a security team to check on any collaborationists who might be spying for the Germans. The previous day, April 10, the Germans had executed 14 civilians (they had been arrested near Hoogeveen on the 9th in reprisal for helping French paras), and the corpses were still lying in a nearby wood. Enraged by the atrocity, De Bollardière asked the Dutch to remove them for burial.

At 1 p.m., a force of about 200 German Fallschirmjäger was seen coming towards Spier down the Assen main road. The French waited until they were 50 metres away and then opened fire. In the sharp battle that ensued, the SAS suffered nine casualties, two of them fatal: Sergeant Claude Campan, the Bren gunner, killed by a bullet in the head, and Major Jean Simon, the battalion second-in-command, wounded in the head after he took over the weapon (he died in a hospital in Hoogeveen that evening). The French were running out of ammunition and about to be overwhelmed when – 'in the best manner of the films' (as the Canadian Official History put it) – armoured cars of the 8th Reconnaissance Regiment arrived and drove away the Germans. It was a timely rescue at a critical moment. As Brigadier Calvert later put it in his report: 'In attacking and taking Spier, De Bollardière showed great offensive spirit but, in view of the size of his party and lightness of his weapons, he did perhaps bite off more than he could chew'.

Soldat Pierre Saunal, a member of Vallières's stick, had volunteered to accompany the Dutchmen who went to recover the murdered civilians and he returned to the crossroads just in time to help stave off the attack:

> 'I went there, it was over a kilometre away. They loaded more than a dozen bodies onto a cart, mostly young men. As I was returning to the crossroads, my comrades signalled me to take cover, because the Germans were coming back. Crawling through a ditch I reached a strongpoint where De Bollardière, Major Simon, Sergeant Campan, and possibly Capitaine Paumier were located. This defence work consisted of a circular hole about four metres in diameter surrounded by a wall, a metre and a half high, made of wood and earth, and was to provide cover for an anti-tank gun. But its top was open, which made it a good target. There were manholes all along the road. The Germans came from the north, walking upright, without taking any special precautions. Campan was in position with the Bren gun. De Bollardière said, "You fire on my orders. Chemin [Soldat Louis Chemin] and I will cover the Bren gunner."
>
> 'When the first Germans were within 50 metres, Bollo shouted, "Fire!" The weapon jammed. Campan reloaded but the Germans, who had seen him, retaliated. They were apparently paratroopers and carried Schmeisser-type sub-machine guns, which have an exceptionally high rate of fire. A bullet hit the Bren gunner square in

Having been relieved in the manner of the US cavalry in the Old West, the SAS troopers relax on the edge of the gun pit. The Dutch girls are (L-R) Geesje Smit, Femmie Smit, Ans (an evacuee from western Holland) and Roelfien Ruben. (Wybo Boersma Collection)

The thatched roof in the background is that of the Zanting farm, which stood across the road from the Cafe Ten Buur. Much altered, it is today the Hotel De Woudzoom. (Karel Margry)

the head, and Major Simon, who took over the weapon, suffered the same fate. Just as German reinforcements were emerging from the woods from the west, the Canadians arrived, causing the Germans to quickly depart. From the ditch, I stretched out my hand, holding my yellow identification scarf as high up as I could without exposing any more of my body. To my right, Sous-Lieutenant Dreyfus emerged from the ditch to do the same, but he was shot in the thigh by a Canadian. The Canadians didn't pursue the enemy but quickly evacuated our wounded. Meanwhile, one of our men had finished off a wounded German in his manhole, much to De Bollardière's annoyance.'

Capitaine Gilbert Paumier (standing left) and men of his stick pictured after the action. The exact location is unsure. (Wybo Boersma Collection)

Capitaine Paumier:

'I was lying next to Major Simon when he was hit in the forehead by a bullet. We were behind an earthwork. When he raised himself to observe the road, he was hit by a rifleman who was in a manhole about 50 metres away from us. I believe the German gunner was himself mortally wounded by Caporal Alexis Beaude.

'Our doctor, Adjutant Pierre Dumas, did all he could with everything he had to treat Simon. Shortly afterwards, at most half an hour later, the Canadians arrived. They immediately evacuated our wounded: Simon, Dreyfus and Caporal Jules Margarit, among others.'

In the far southern end of the 3ème RCP zone lay one of 'Amherst''s main objectives, the Luftwaffe airfield at Steenwijk-Havelte. The 3ème Squadron had assigned two of its five sticks to secure it. One of them, No. 17 commanded by Lieutenant Yves Gayard, on assembly found that two men were missing and one other had broken his ankle in the jump. Also, they had landed five kilometres too far to the north-east, near the village of Ruinen, so they started making their way south-westward. Early next morning, April 9, they de-mined a sluice bridge over the Hoogeveense Vaart, cutting the cables and dropping the aircraft bombs in the water. Shortly after, two Canadian scout cars of the 18th Armoured Car Regiment (12th Manitoba Dragoons) arrived from the south and asked them to guard the bridge for the night.

Next morning, mounted on the armoured vehicles, Gayard's men went to reconnoitre the airfield. However, they found it pitted with bomb craters and totally unusable. One of Gayard's men, Sergeant Roger Flamand, recalled the action:

Just as had happened elsewhere in Europe, 'Amherst' saw regular warfare mixed with the settling of scores between patriots and Nazi collaborators. A particularly dark incident occurred outside the small village of Punthorst, in the far south-western corner of the 'Amherst' area, on April 8. Two sticks of the 3ème Squadron of the 3ème RCP, No. 15 under Sous-Lieutenant Jacques Bouffartigue and No. 16 under Aspirant Gérard Lagallarde, had landed south of the village and joined up with a resistance group under Jos Bonvanie. After consultation, they decided to arrest the several families living in the area that were members of the Dutch Nazi party NSB. Two men, Soldat Yves Loichot from Bouffartigue's stick and Dutch resistant Kees de Roos, went on a motorbike to arrest three families. As they arrived at the farm of the Santing family at No. 16 Dekkersweg *(above)*, the three sons of the family, all NSB landwachters (militiamen), entrenched themselves in the house, opening fire on their opponents from a first-floor window. Loichot and De Roos, who had taken cover in the ditch across the road, were both killed by a bullet in the head. A girl next-door, Lenie Spijkerman, sped to the Staatsbossen woods to inform the SAS paras of what had happened. When Caporal-Chef Raoul Loichot heard of the death of his twin brother he, together with Sergeant Jacques Noël and a few resistance men, immediately went to the farm. Entering the house, they heard noise in the hayloft and riddled it with fire. Four men – the three Santing brothers, Jacob, Willem and Harm, and their father Hendrik – staggered out, bleeding from multiple wounds, and were finished off on the spot. But this was not the end of the bloodshed. That evening, enraged by the loss of their compatriot, Jos Bonvanie and his resistance group executed four others: Hendrik Santing's wife, two members of another arrested NSB family (Klaas and Rutger Prins) and the son of third family, 15-year-old Alex Duif. Within a few hours ten people had died. (Karel Margry)

'Finally, we reach the southern edge of the airfield. We have to cross a large meadow. The armoured cars stay behind the last clumps of trees and provide us with cover for that final jump by firing smoke grenades. At the far end of the meadow runs a canal. There's no bridge. A small boat lies moored on the far bank. A little further on, among the trees, is a small farmhouse with a thatched roof. You can see that soldiers have set up some fortifications in the terrain: trenches and approach trenches barely 50 meters away; but not a shot is fired and there's not a soul in sight. How are we supposed to cross the canal other than swimming or using a raft? I and a few men walk upright for a long time along the road that runs alongside the canal when finally a dirty handkerchief is waved above a parapet. We shout an order in German: "Komm! Schnell! Hände hoch!" Fourteen unarmed men suddenly appear and walk to the high bank near the boat.

Shortly after liberation, two white crosses were erected where Yves Loichot (seen *above* on the right with his brother Raoul on the left) and Kees de Roos *(right)* had fallen.

'We're still shouting "Komm! Schnell!" All Germans quickly climb into the boat, nearly making it capsize. They row like madmen, to no avail. We burst out laughing: they have forgotten to cast off the mooring line. While we begin frisking and questioning them, I with three or four soldiers cross to the other bank. We walk to the trench and a light shiver still grips us: for half an hour we've been walking right in front of a magnificent machine gun with ammunition belt fed in, and a Panzerfaust and a lot of rifles lie a little further away. When we question a Gefreiter to find out if the runways are still in good condition and if the Germans haven't sabotaged them, he says: "Why should we sabotage them? The runways have been unusable since the last RAF raids." We begin to wonder what we're doing there. Shortly afterwards, a series of dull thuds from 88mm shells erupts in our area. From our prisoners we learn that a battery of these guns has indeed been left behind in the area.

'That afternoon, having reached the farmhouse across the canal and with everything quieted down, there was a new alarm. A sudden burst of fire from automatic weapons, voices shouting, "The Boche are coming back!" and shooting beginning from all sides. In vain, I asked, "But where are they then? I haven't seen a single one." And then the farmhouse, hit by tracer fire and incendiary rounds, began

Eight days later, on April 16, Loichot and De Roos were buried in the town of Meppel. Here the cortege passes through Weerdstraat on its way from the Stephanus Church to the Hesselingen Cemetery. Leading the procession (and wearing a paratrooper's helmet) is Jos Bonvanie. (Wybo Boersma Collection)

A tranquil street, unchanged in over eight decades. (Karel Margry)

The procession entering the small cemetery.

Still a secluded little burial ground on the edge of Meppel today.
(Karel Margry)

to burn. We re-crossed the canal to the other bank. That evening the Canadians came to pick us up.'

In adding the aerodrome to the list of targets for 'Amherst', No. 84 Group intelligence had badly fouled up, overlooking the fact that 114 B-17s of the US Eighth Air Force had dropped 271 tons of high-explosive on it on March 24, completely destroying the runway. With the Allies now so near, the Germans completed destruction by wholescale demolitions that continued until the 12th, then abandoned the airfield.

Jos Bonvanie pays his respect at the grave of Yves Loichot.

Loichot no longer lies at Meppel as his remains were transferred to the French military cemetery at Kapelle in the south-western Netherlands in 1949. The cold-blooded shootings at Punthorst were judicially investigated by the Dutch and French authorities after the war. The resistance men who had executed their fellow-countrymen were sentenced to three months in 1952 but they never served time, the charges being dismissed. The SAS veterans were questioned by the French police but never prosecuted. (Karel Margry)

The stick that came down furthest south in the 3ème RCP area was that of Lieutenant Pierre Baratin. It landed just south of Balkbrug, a crossroad village on the Ommen to Meppel road. Their main action was sabotaging the Meppel to Zwolle railway line and stopping an enemy train. Here, members of the stick pose for a snapshot with two local girls at Balkbrug. Standing (L-R): Soldats Antoine Murati and Octave Bernault, Caporal Robert Prévost, an unnamed Dutch girl, Soldat Henri Lagarde and a Dutch girl that acted as a guide. Kneeling: Soldat Antoine Padovani.
(Wybo Boersma Collection)

Today, the old Ommen to Meppel road is only a minor connection whereas the lateral road through Balkbrug has become the dual-carriage N377 Zwolle to Coevorden highway. This is looking westwards down Zwolseweg.
(Karel Margry)

The same men and girls posing at the local windmill. (Wybo Boersma Collection)

Locally known as De Star, the mill stood on Molenweg just east of the main village crossroads but by 1974 it stood so surrounded by high buildings that it was moved a few hundred metres further east to a new location more out in the open. (Karel Margry)

The sticks that had landed in the southern zones were also the first to link up with the ground forces, scout cars of the 12th Manitoba Dragoons already reaching Balkbrug on April 8. The Canadian main force reached the village three days later. Here Kangaroos of the 1st Armoured Personnel Carrier Regiment and Sherman tanks of the 10th Armoured Regiment (The Fort Garry Horse) queue up in the canal-lined village street. (LAC DND 49757)

Time has brought few changes to Ommerweg. (Karel Margry)

Canadian Army photographer Lieutenant Daniel Guravich pictured French paratroops who 'beat the Canadians to Balkbrug by a few days' talking to the Kangaroo crews. (LAC DND 49756)

THE END OF THE OPERATION

THE CONTACT ESTABLISHED BY the 12th Manitoba Dragoons on the early morning of April 9 was one of the first meetings between the ground forces of Canadian II Corps and the French SAS. The very first link-up had occurred the day before, April 8, when a section of four armoured Jeeps of the 5th (Belgian) SAS Battalion, operating out of Coevorden, contacted a stick – No. 4 of the 2ème RCP under Lieutenant Jean Sriber – that had been dropped so far south that they landed near Dedemsvaart, south of the Hoogeveense Vaart. By April 10 the Canadian armoured cars had still contacted only about 70 parachutists (four sticks) in the Meppel area.

It had been assumed that the SAS troops would be reached by ground forces in not more than 72 hours, hence they had landed with rations for only three days. However, when this period was about to expire on the 10th, only about a quarter of the French paras had yet been overrun. Considering whether he should ask his troops to fight their way back to friendly lines, Brigadier Calvert, who was still superintending the operation from First Canadian Army Headquarters, decided against this, as this would mean coming out in the open, crossing canals, etc. Instead he ordered that sticks with casualties or in difficulties were to lie low and await relief, and that the others should continue to harass the enemy. To increase the chances of relief, he asked General Crerar, the commander of First Canadian Army, to deflect part of the 1st Polish Armoured Division west into the 'Amherst' area. The Army Commander however decided that he would not be justified in diverting an important part of his force from its main object in order to save what was comparatively a small unit, particularly as food was reported to be plentiful where they were operating; and Calvert, in retrospect, agreed that his judgement had been sound.

Despite Crerar's negative decision, a part of the Polish division did veer north-west into the 'Amherst' area. Early on April 10, the 10th Mounted Rifles, the division's armoured reconnaissance regiment, supported by a squadron of the 10th Dragoons Motor Battalion and a troop of M10 tank destroyers from the 1st Anti-Tank Regiment, set off north-westwards from Coevorden 'to rescue some paratroops who, having completed their mission, were in a very precarious situation behind the enemy lines'. At 1 p.m. they reached Witteveen, south-east of Westerbork, where they found the group of the 2ème RCP under Major Puech-Samson, by now 64 strong. Mounted

The 5th (Belgian) SAS Battalion had started their own operation, code-named 'Larkswood', on the right flank of their French colleagues, operating with Jeep teams ahead of the Canadian 4th Armoured Division. From April 8, they ventured into the 'Amherst' area to find and link up with the French parachutists. The day before, one of their Jeeps, named *Arthur* and manned by Sergeant Georges d'Oultremont, Corporal Michel Mas and Private Jaques Oosters was pictured in Ane, a hamlet eight kilometres south-west of Coevorden.

They had halted at the junction of De Vaart and De Steeghe on the edge of the village. This is the same spot today, looking east down De Vaart.
(Reitze Bierma)

on the decks of the Cromwell tanks, the SAS men were brought back to Coevorden.

Lieutenant Mikolaj Antonowicz commanded the tank destroyers that were part of the Polish task force. He recalled:

> 'We didn't know exactly where the French were but only had a message specifying the area where we would likely find them. To cover as much ground as possible, we set off at daybreak in three columns along three parallel axes, heading towards Westerbork.

On April 10, the 1st Polish Armoured Division sent a task force into the 'Amherst' area from Coevorden, the 10th Mounted Rifles and the 10th Dragoons Motor Battalion despatching three mixed columns to contact the SAS paratroopers. Around noon, No. 1 Squadron of the 10th Mounted Rifles reached the group of the 2ème RCP under battalion commander Major Puech-Samson at the Witteveen woods (see page 9). Mounting the squadron's Cromwell tanks, the 64 SAS men were brought to Coevorden, where the SAS troops were to rendezvous after relief. At the village of Dalen, halfway there, Puech-Samson (centre) stopped to talk with the 10th Mounted Rifles commander, Major Jerzy Wasilewski (right), on top of the latter's command tank. (Wybo Boersma Collection)

The meeting over, Puech-Samson climbs down from the Cromwell, while a Dutchman chalks another greeting on the rear of the tank. (Wybo Boersma Collection)

'Somewhere on the banks of the Oranjekanaal we were fortunate enough to find a few of the parachutists. We had to act quickly because, according to the information received, they wouldn't be able to withstand attacks from enemy forces, which were stronger and larger than them, for long. The area they were in was flat, with little vegetation. Crisscrossed by a network of canals and a labyrinth of roads, dikes and bridges, most of which had been destroyed by the enemy, it was extremely unsuitable for the advance of tanks. The German command, once again demonstrating its lack of imagination, therefore hadn't fortified it with very effective anti-tank defences. For

Once they became available on the third day of the operation, the SAS Jeeps did yeoman service in reinforcing the parachute sticks, evacuating their wounded and sending out long-range patrols. By April 13, Jeep Platoon Betbèze was operating well north of the original 'Amherst' area, fighting with the Canadian forward troops east of Groningen. This is Jeep M5834315, which we earlier saw at Rolde (see page 64), pictured at the village of Noordbroek on April 15. In the back are Aspirant Edmé and Soldat Le Chevalier, and looking into the camera is Soldat Thonnerieux.
(Wybo Boersma Collection)

They stood parked on Markt, the village square, but both houses seen in the wartime photo have since disappeared. All that remains is the house beyond, the former village teacher's house, now the local library.
(Wybo Boersma)

us this mistake was an advantage but for the hunted parachutists it was an even bigger stroke of luck.

'The absence of 88mm guns, in particular, allowed us to take risks and advance faster than anticipated. Thanks to our tank guns, 12.7mm machine guns, and other light machine guns, we quickly destroyed all resistance nests that had been set up along the dikes or near the bridges. The main obstacle remained the terrain, where the tanks could sometimes only advance along narrow roads, which collapsed under their weight. From time to time, the Cromwell tanks, as if amphibious, took a narrow canal at full speed, sending enormous fountains of muddy water into the air. Sometimes they crossed roads and drove straight through soaking fields, while others balanced like tightrope walkers on overly narrow dikes.

'So we continued our way, carefully searching everywhere for the parachutists. Time was of the essence and we had to hurry, which was best for them and for us, before we were cut off from our rear. After all, we had penetrated deep into enemy lines, without communication with our main force. I think we benefited from the surprise of the Germans, who were discomfited by our completely unexpected action with armoured troops and had to interpret it as a harbinger of our full-scale offensive on this front.

By April 17, Jeep platoon Betbèze had returned south and was in Westerbork, and later that day went to Groningen to look for 33 Allied POWs who had been reported passing through the city the day before. It is unknown where this picture was taken but in the Jeep are Sergeant Bernard Carry (from stick No. 11 of the 2ème RCP) and Mr. Reijntjes, a Dutchman who was probably serving as the platoon's guide and interpreter. (Wybo Boersma Collection)

The platoon was accompanied in Westerbork by a Canadian armoured car and five Canadian Bren carriers and supported by members of several sticks who had congregated in the village. Here Lieutenant Michel de Camaret, commander of the 2ème Squadron (and leader of stick No. 8) of the 2ème RCP, stands with Caporal Jean-Paul Klein (front right) and Soldat Dominique Quennouelle, both from stick No. 7, at one of the carriers. (Wybo Boersma Collection)

'After forcing our way through with cannon fire, neutralising several strongpoints equipped with automatic weapons and a few small-calibre anti-tank guns, and destroying several companies of dug-in infantry in their trenches, we arrived in Westerbork around noon, where we found the remnants of the French parachutists. They were scattered, completely exhausted, shivering from cold and fatigue, and almost out of food.

'For the most part they were truly at the end of their strength. They were short of ammunition and sleep and could not hold out much longer against a strong and well-organised enemy. I will long remember their unit commander [Major Puech-Samson], dirty as he was, unshaven, exhausted, with red-rimmed eyes from fatigue and lack of sleep, but displaying an indomitable fighting spirit and the will to die rather than surrender. He told us that he'd been hearing the gunfire getting closer since 10 a.m. and that he was praying to God that it was us coming with our tanks, and not the Germans. His men were decimated; only 64 men remained in that sector, and he had no idea what had happened to the ones that were missing.'

Anticipating the return of paras that had been overrun, and with Steenwijk airfield (the originally planned rendezvous point) unusable, Colonel Prendergast and a small staff had on April 9 set up a small headquarters, known as Tac 20 Liaison, at Coevorden in readiness to receive them, evacuate wounded, and arrange for their return to the UK.

With the cancellation of the Jeep drop, SAS Main HQ had immediately started organising to bring the Jeeps to Holland in other ways. Ten of them were flown over to the Continent on April 8 and they arrived at Prendergast's headquarters at Coevorden on the 10th. Manned with personnel from sticks that had already been overrun, they were organised in platoons of two or three vehicles, eight of the Jeeps going to the 2ème RCP and two to the 3ème. Starting on April 11, they sent out search patrols to the north and north-west, locating and bringing back missing sticks and evacuating wounded. Several of the Jeeps had encounters with German troops and came back with prisoners. One Jeep party went as far north as Groningen in a vain search for SAS troops that had been reported marching through the city as POWs.

Lieutenant Denys Cochin, leader of stick No. 22 of the 2ème RCP, posing in one of the carriers among the jubilant Dutch. (Wybo Boersma Collection)

The French were helped in this task by their colleagues of the 5th (Belgian) SAS Battalion. Some 280 strong and equipped with 33 armoured Jeeps and several 15cwt lorries mounting 3-inch mortars, they had already reached Coevorden with the Canadian 4th Armoured Division on the 6th, but then had to wait until the arrival of the 1st Polish Armoured Division before they could start their planned role of operating ahead of the armour (Operation 'Larkswood'). On April 9, one of their Jeep platoons already shortly contacted Puech-Samson's group, then still at its base in the Witteveen wood, who reported their casualties from the Westerbork raid but said they needed no further help. On the 11th, another Jeep platoon drove out to Orvelte and rescued a group from the 2ème RCP that was fighting in the Schoonloo woods.

Brigadier Calvert, the SAS Brigade commander, had decided to join the Belgians in their push to find the French paras. He recalled:

> 'Four hundred men is not much of a force to take into a hostile area of that size, even if certain key places have already been captured by the advance party, as in this case. I therefore decided to fall back again on bluff, which had seen me through some difficult situations

Coevorden lies close to the Dutch-German border and, as they waited for the other sticks to dribble in after relief, few of the SAS men could resist making a short trip to set foot on enemy soil. These men were pictured at the bridge over the Vechte river at Laar, a small village just across the border south-east of Coevorden, captured by the Canadians on April 5. As evidenced by the white flags, the roadblock had not been defended. The uniformed German is a customs officer. (Wybo Boersma Collection)

The bridge has been replaced by a modern version. This is the road entering the village from the south. (Karel Margry)

in the past. I had been sent a large, impressive-looking staff car and reckoned that most Germans would think twice before firing at it, simply because it was not the sort of vehicle one expected to see actually in action. And before they could realise they had been tricked the Belgians, following up, could deal with them.

'It was a makeshift scheme which didn't bear too much thinking about so we put it into action before we could change our minds. I took a driver with me and one of my staff captains, a red-haired, French-speaking officer with the wonderful name of Potter Miller Mundy. We stuck a large Union Jack on the front of the car and set off, hoping for the best. I was already feeling a little more confident because we had also managed to take with us a Polish battery of self-propelled 25-pounders, which would be invaluable if we hit a really determined bunch of Germans.

'As we drove through the flat Dutch countryside Potter Miller Mundy and I were feeling pretty scared, to say the least. But to our

After a few days, the SAS troops were brought to Nijmegen, there to await air transport back to Britain. Soldat Albert Rambeau and Caporal-Chef Maurice Layral of Lieutenant Duno's stick No. 12 of the 3ème RCP *(left)* and Caporal Paul Le Guilly of Sous-Lieutenant Henry Corta's stick No. 10 of the 2ème RCP *(right)* all had their picture taken on Keizer-Karel-Plein, the large roundabout square in the centre of town. (Wybo Boersma Collection)

amazement the plan worked like a charm. We would drive into a village and the Dutch, seeing this big British staff car and the Union Jack, would dash out to greet us. First among them would be the Resistance and they would quickly deal with any Germans who looked as if they might turn nasty; most of the enemy troops surrendered to us. They were a pretty poor lot in most cases. The crack units were further south in the main battle areas and many of the ones we picked up were little more than occupation force.

'The French parachutists were pleased to see us and I would leave a few of the Belgians at each place to reinforce them until the Canadians took over. At one village a French corporal rushed out to greet us, obviously relieved at our arrival, and got very excited when he saw me. "Attendez, mon general, attendez!", he shouted, and dashed back into a nearby house. A moment

The same view at the turnoff to Groesbeek today. (Karel Margry)

Sergeant Bernard Carry (lower left) and friends from Aspirant Edmé's stick No. 11 of the 3ème RCP. From the third day of the operation onwards, they had crewed two vehicles of Jeep Platoon Betbèze. (Wybo Boersma Collection)

They were in Molenstraat, the street that runs into the heart of Nijmegen from the Keizer-Karel-Plein.
(Karel Margry)

later he ran again carrying something in his hand and with a tremendous flourish and a happy smile presented me with a pheasant!'

By April 14, the Canadian 2nd Infantry Division had wholly passed through the 'Amherst' area and had started the battle for Groningen (which would prove difficult and last for four days). This meant that all of the SAS troops had been overrun and indeed by the 15th – eight days after the start of the operation – most of those not killed or taken prisoner had reported in. On being assembled at Coevorden, the SAS troops were moved back to Nijmegen, there to await air transport back to the UK. It took some time to arrange aircraft but by April 21, 14 days after their take-off to Holland, the majority of the French SAS were back at their base camps near Ipswich.

'Amherst' had been quite costly for both sides. As for casualties inflicted on the enemy, the two SAS battalions claimed a total of 269 killed, 70 wounded, 150 killed or wounded but unconfirmed, and 187 taken prisoner. In material damage they claimed 29 enemy vehicles destroyed or captured and three railway lines cut. (The actual number of Germans killed was much lower, about 40).

French losses added up to 33 killed, 35 wounded and 92 missing – a grand total of 160, meaning a loss rate of nearly 23 per cent. All of the 92 missing had in fact been taken prisoner. Most ended up in northern Germany, the wounded in a Kriegsmarine hospital in Wesermünde near Bremerhaven, many others first in the Sandbostel POW camp, from which on April 16 they were transferred to the Milag-Marlag internment camp at Westertimke near Bremen, where another group had already arrived on the 14th. Here, 67 of them were liberated on April 28. The wounded were not liberated until May 7.

It is difficult to make a precise assessment of Operation 'Amherst'. The Canadian commanders, Crerar and Simonds, seemed satisfied with its results; General Gale of I British Airborne Corps and Brigadier Calvert were full of praise. Gale considered that the effect on enemy morale was 'considerable' and concluded that 'numerous troops who were badly needed for defence against advancing ground forces had to be deployed over a very wide area against these French regiments.' There was much criticism on the planning

Soldat Albert Frantz and Caporal-Chef Guy Pasquet from Major Puech-Samson's stick at the big road bridge over the Waal river, one of the main targets of that other airborne undertaking in the Netherlands, Operation 'Market-Garden', of seven months earlier. (Wybo Boersma Collection)

The famous bridge today. (Karel Margry)

On April 20, air transport became available and the SAS men were taken to Eindhoven aerodrome (Allied airfield B-78) where Dakotas of No. 46 Group stood waiting. The remnants of stick No. 20 of the 2ème RCP posed for a last snapshot on the runway before take-off to RAF Woodbridge in Suffolk: (L-R) Lieutenant André Varnier, Sergeant-Chef Paul Golder, two unidentified men (either Sergeant Manuel Olivier, Caporal André Le Bihan or Soldat Emile Coriton), Sergeant Roger Berteloot and Soldat Charles Schweitzer. (Wybo Boersma Collection)

and preparation of the operation, especially among French commanders and junior officers, but in general the execution was judged a success. However, the question remains whether the Canadian advance would have been any slower without the use of the SAS troops. With the Germans being as disorganised as they were, it probably did not make much difference.

The main memorial to Operation 'Amherst' is the French SAS monument in Assen. Located on the corner of Balkenweg and Oude Hoofdvaartsweg, it was dedicated on the 40th anniversary of 'Amherst' in April 1985. A plaque on the monument records the names of all 33 men of the 2ème and 3ème RCPs that fell in the operation. (Karel Margry)